a mother's heart
MOVED THE
HAND OF GOD

a mother's heart MOVED THE HAND OF GOD

TEDD GALLOWAY

NEW YORK

a mother's heart MOVED THE HAND OF GOD

Published in New York, New York, by Morgan James Publishing. Morgan James and The Entrepreneurial Publisher are trademarks of Morgan James, LLC. www.MorganJamesPublishing.com

The Morgan James Speakers Group can bring authors to your live event. For more information or to book an event visit The Morgan James Speakers Group at www.TheMorganJamesSpeakersGroup.com.

FREE eBook edition for your existing eReader with purchase

PRINT NAME ABOVE

For more information, instructions, restrictions, and to register your copy, go to **www.bitlit.ca/readers/register** or use your QR Reader to scan the barcode:

ISBN 978-1-61448-678-7 paperback
ISBN 978-1-61448-679-4 eBook
ISBN 978-1-61448-680-0 audio
ISBN 978-1-61448-950-4 hardcover
Library of Congress Control Number:
2013949920

Cover Design by:
Chris Treccani
www.3dogdesign.net

Interior Design by:
Bonnie Bushman
bonnie@caboodlegraphics.com

In an effort to support local communities, raise awareness and funds, Morgan James Publishing donates a percentage of all book sales for the life of each book to Habitat for Humanity Peninsula and Greater Williamsburg.

Get involved today, visit
www.MorganJamesBuilds.com.

Habitat
for Humanity
Peninsula and
Greater Williamsburg
Building Partner

this is dedicated to:

God, for Life and Light; Donna, my wife, for living the truth;
My three daughters in their example of love;

My family at large, we will always have each other;

The healing of the wounded who remain
faithful to God and their faith community.

Contents

acknowledgments

A special thanks to:

Joe Brisson who worked on the audio version and laughed with me;
Roger Phillips who worked with me on the manuscript and helped me
learn to discover; Mike Carter for prayer and good words;
Lewie and Laurie Rohl who are choice friends and a rich blessing;
Friendships that are spread across the globe:
Ossineke United Methodist Church,
First Baptist Church of Lincoln, Morenci United Methodist Church,
Heart connections in every church we served,

Wonderful brothers and sisters we left behind in Zambia,
we hope to see you again one day.

introduction

S he weighed about four pounds, and her fragile body could fit in just one of my hands. With her little head cradled in my fingertips, her bottom would be resting on the lower part of my palm. How could such a weak and sick child survive? The ugly claw of malnutrition and disease had already snatched away millions of infants in the Southern African regions. Years of drought had left hundreds of square miles as parched, lifeless land and put untold thousands in their village graves. Even though she had survived two days, this child would be no different. The malnutrition that laid waste her mother had left its ugly effect upon the infant as well. The few drops of water that were dribbled into her mouth were filled with parasites, and they were now invading her digestive system. If the malnutrition alone didn't kill her, than the parasites would help.

The words from the doctor seemed cold, yet they were words that had been used scores of times before. The matter-of-fact tone was not meant to hurt, just reveal the history he had lived. "Put her aside and let her slip away." These were the words he spoke but were never listened to. Donna was not about to let any baby "just slip away."

This is the story of a mother's heart moved to embrace struggling and dying infants in a land overrun by disease and death. It is the story of a spirit determined to survive in spite of staggering obstacles. But most important of all, this is the story of God's love and power beautifully displayed in a mother's care and a child's metamorphosis into a vibrant life.

Have you ever struggled with the question of why things happen at a certain time? Have you ever doubted or questioned the timing of God? This is the story of God's timing. His handprint is visible in every event. In some of the events His imprint is easy to see. In some of the tragedies that took place it is like a fingerprint left behind. We recognize it after the events have taken place.

There were times during these events that I questioned the timing and compassion of God. I believe that many of you who read these words will understand what I am saying. My prayer for everybody who reads this is simple; may our Father, the God of all love and compassion, move in your heart so that you may understand the power that is unleashed when you love people as His Spirit leads you. I believe that it is time for the church of Jesus Christ to do more than profess with our mouths that we love God and each other. There are people all around us who are the walking dead. They are waiting and longing for the love of God to bring life and vitality to their diseased and malformed existence.

ready, set, go

$\wedge\wedge\wedge$

We had been waiting ten years for this day. It was early March when the long awaited envelope arrived. I was holding in my hand the letter from our denomination in Zambia. We were going to a bush station named Kankata, located about two hours from the capital city of Lusaka.

Very early in our life together Donna and I knew that God was leading us to serve Him outside the bounds of our country. At the age of twelve, Donna felt the call of God upon her heart to become a missionary nurse. The realization came to both of us one Sunday evening. As a married couple we were involved in our little congregation in Northeast Michigan. We led the Sunday school openings and taught Sunday school classes. One Sunday night, former missionaries were coming to do a missions presentation. As a couple they had served in a remote school and hospital in Northern Rhodesia, soon to become Zambia. They talked about the love and joy the Tonga people displayed, about how important it was for children to get a good education. And they talked about how God was helping the people survive every day in a very poor land. At the end of their presentation they challenged everyone to support the missions as well as they possibly could. Donna and I felt in our hearts that we needed to talk with them. After talking with us for some time, they encouraged us to be faithful and to trust God to open the doors to the places He had planned for us.

A short while later, we entered our denomination's college for ordination. Both of us would be ordained into the ministry. During that two-year period of intense education God provided gentle reminders of His call upon our lives. After our ordination, as we served our churches, we waited for God to open the doors for us. Each year at the time of our review we would remind the administration that we were seeking to fulfill our calling to missionary service. Many times our leaders would encourage us to wait on God's perfect timing. A couple of times we wondered what God was doing. Why did we have to wait so long? Did He just want us to be willing, and that was our challenge? During these years we always made it a point to talk with the girls about serving God, first to Marily and then to Hilary. We tried to do it in simple ways that they could understand. We wanted them to know that God was leading us into an exciting adventure. We wanted them to know that wherever we lived our Heavenly Father had led us to our new home.

Well, the day after holding the letter in my hand we had a meeting with our congregation. Our denominational leader came and spoke with our folks about the future for us and for them. It was a very tearful and yet exciting time for us. He told us that we would stay at our church until the end of June, and then we would use the next two months to prepare for our journey. The very next week we began getting tons, or so it seemed, of information. We were informed of all of the inoculations that were required, and we made immediate arrangements to begin getting the required shots. It would take eight to twelve weeks to get all of them. At times our arms and rears would be so sore it would be hard to take the twenty-mile ride home. We received information from Zambia explaining what life was like and what we must bring. A week after holding onto that letter things were happening so fast it was like we were caught in a whirlwind.

How do you prepare to move a family halfway around the world? The list of what we needed to take was staggering. We were told it was easy. Just take everything you will need for the next four years of your family's life. We would have to take clothing to last four years. We also needed to take every non-available food item we wanted, as well as anything we wanted to help us celebrate the holidays, even Christmas cards and wrapping paper. And finally, we were to take everything to outfit our house, except the furniture, of course.

How do you estimate how much your children are going to grow? Marily was fifteen and almost 5'10" tall. If Hilary grew like her sister, we wouldn't be able to keep clothes on her. We sat down and worked on a list for our clothes. I thought that I would need at least twenty pairs of pants along with Sunday clothing. I would equal that number with shirts, socks, and underwear. Donna's list was similar in number to mine. The plan that we worked for the girls seemed feasible. They would take enough to last for two years, taking into consideration normal growth. At the end of two years we would be coming home for some vacation time, so at that time we would get them enough to last for the next two years.

By Labor Day, we had everything purchased that we thought we would need. Right after Labor Day the shipping company was coming to pick up our supplies. I had built five shipping containers about five-foot cubed. Inside the boxes was everything we needed to begin our life in the Zambian bush. In one box we put everything needed for our kitchen, from pots and pans to the dishtowels. In one container I packed the girls' bicycles with blankets and sleeping bags stuffed around them, hoping they would be kept safe during the transit. Another container held our meager holiday supplies. We had a small artificial Christmas tree along with some lights and decorations. Also, we very carefully packed our favorite angel tree topper. Another container had cases of instant noodles, macaroni and cheese, coffee, instant drink mixes, boxes of salt and pepper and other spices. We also had rechargeable batteries of every size with two chargers. We would need to remember to put all of our seeds for the garden in our suitcases, for it was made very clear that we would have to plant our garden as soon as we arrived. That garden would be our food lifeline during the first months of our new life.

Just a few days after the shipping company picked up our belongings, we received our departure information. We would fly out of Chicago to Amsterdam. After about a ten-or twelve-hour rest we would head to Nairobi, Kenya and then on to Zambia. The flights would take two days and be about twenty hours in the air. We had approximately one week to get a hold of family members and prepare for the departure. The next few days it was hard to keep our feet on the ground.

Just a couple of days before departure some disturbing thoughts came back to us. They were the same thoughts we dealt with when we heard we were finally going. What if something happened to Donna's mother, Marily and Hilary's only grandma? Donna might be able to come home, but nobody else would be able to. What if something happened to one of the girls? What would Grandma do? She could never travel to Zambia. She was sixty-nine and living on a very small Social Security pension. But despite those misgivings, our hearts settled as we remembered that we were in God's hands, as was our entire family.

Our day of departure arrived. The tickets were in order, all of our travel documents secure and our bags packed. It was time to leave. We left our small apartment and headed to the airport. We were so excited it is impossible to put it into words. Marily and Hilary had visions of wild animals and adventures. Donna was overcome with the truth that she was going to be living out her calling to serve in Africa. I was swimming in thoughts of what had to be done and how this was going to change my family. At the airport everybody gathered around as we prepared to pray and board the flight. Our suitcases had been checked through, and now it was just the four of us. We were ready to board our flight to adventure. Donna and the girls passed around tearful farewell hugs. The most difficult was saying goodbye to Grandma; Marily and Hilary loved her so much. She taught them how to bake chocolate chip cookies and pick wild berries. They laughed every time they talked about the big grasshopper that jumped up Grandma's dress when they were out picking wild berries. We had our prayer together, and the Galloway family ventured off to Africa.

We boarded the plane and headed off across the Atlantic Ocean to the Netherlands. The girls had never flown before. This would be quite an experience for them. We told them that they would be experiencing a lifestyle that 99 percent of Americans would never have. From this first plane trip to living in the bush I sensed we would experience things that we would never forget. I also knew the experiences would change the way we thought about the world and how blessed America was.

The first leg of the trip was long. It took about ten hours to get to Amsterdam. We arrived early the next morning. After clearing customs and checking our precious luggage, we left the airport. We made arrangements to spend ten or twelve hours at a small hotel near the square in downtown Amsterdam. Standing outside the terminal, I flagged down a taxi. As soon as he loaded up our bags and I told him where we were going, his foot was glued to the gas pedal. I don't think it came up off the floor until he hit the brakes pulling into the hotel. I had heard of crazy taxi drivers before, but this was like comparing a formula one driver to a go-cart driver. More than once Donna grabbed on to my arm, like I was going to make this speed-addicted machine slow down. Hilary, on the other hand, loved every second of the asphalt-trapped flight.

We checked in at the little hotel and settled for just a bit. After a short time we wanted to explore this marvelous city. Visions of windmills and Hans Brinker filled my mind. We walked around the small shops. At one shop Donna bought a beautiful piece of lace for her mother. She also picked up a couple of pieces of ceramic ware for her mom. I stopped at a small cafe and tried an espresso. After drinking it I knew I would be up for some time. When we headed back to the motel, it was just beginning to get dark. As the streets grew darker, so did the merchandise that the vendors were bringing out onto the sidewalks. We moved past them with the girls as quickly as we could. The permissiveness of the Dutch people was very disturbing.

It was time to head back to the airport. The taxi ride back did not even compare to the first one. We had to recheck our luggage. It was kept in a storage area for us prior to the flight. Just the task of lugging eight suitcases and our bags was exhausting. I took two of the biggest suitcases and a carry-on bag. Donna and the girls each struggled with two of their own plus a carry-on bag. I don't know how my two wonderful daughters did it. It must have been the adrenaline of the entire trip that kept them going. We checked our tickets and boarded the flight to Nairobi. This part of the flight was through the night darkness as was the first part to Amsterdam. It was expected to take about eight hours to arrive in Nairobi.

The flight was smooth, yet we were becoming exhausted. The impact of the emotional experiences coupled with the physical tiredness was showing. As we landed in Nairobi, we knew that we would not be leaving the airport. The layover time was only an hour or so. As I watched the bags, the girls went to use the restroom. They came back with a very sickly look on their faces. They told me the bathrooms were disgusting. Well, I had to use the men's room, so I got my first experience in third-world restroom environments. Without going into all the details, it is enough to say that the bathroom had more roaches running on the walls than I could count.

We had made arrangements with a friend to meet us at the airport. She had been in Kenya for a couple of months. We exchanged some gifts. She brought us cold orange sodas, and we gave her a gift package from her mom.

Finally, the last leg of our journey was about to begin. We were to take a Zambian Airways flight to Lusaka. The flight of fifteen hundred miles would be over rather quickly and at last, we would be arriving at our new home. As soon as we boarded the flight, the stifling heat lay over us like a blanket. I thought things would cool off as soon as the engines started and the air conditioning kicked in. When the flight was about to begin, the pilot made his usual announcements over the PA system. He apologized for the malfunctioning air conditioning system. He hoped that it would function during the flight. Well, it didn't seem to, and we cooked most of the time. At least we were airborne and on our way. It wasn't long into the flight that the heat and the smell of jet fumes began to make us nauseous. When we were asked if we wanted to eat, we politely declined. For the next few hours we simply endured the sultry high flying airbus, knowing we were close to home.

Our landing in Lusaka didn't come soon enough. I was so proud of the girls; they hardly complained and kept a great attitude, even in the heat and discomfort. We gathered our luggage and headed for the immigration processing area. I was about to learn my first lesson about Zambian culture: do not ever be in a hurry; don't hurry to get something done, and don't be in a hurry to get someplace. After standing in line for what seemed like hours, we got to the immigration desk. I gave the officer all of our customs documents: passports and immunization records. After looking the documents over, he opened each passport to the section that contains the pages to be stamped when leaving and entering any country. He very carefully opened his stamp pad on his desk. He slammed his stamp on the pad, and then, *wham*, he slammed the stamp down on the passport. I almost laughed, it all seemed so theatrical. Each passport deserved the same attention, and he performed the same ritual. My second lesson in less than an hour: stamps and stamp pads reveal status in a country where good jobs are rare.

After clearing immigration, we met the man who was taking us to Kankata. He helped us with the bags, and we were ready to go. His truck was waiting just outside the entrance doors. I was thinking, "Let's just jump in and get going." We were tired and dirty and wanted to get to our new home. I handed the luggage to him and he piled it on the back of the truck. The truck was already fully loaded with all kinds of boxes. Lesson three: in such a short time, every truck is loaded to twice its capacity. Every trip was expensive, and there were always supplies to be transported. Well, he tied on the four bags and eight suitcases. He seemed to use a mile of rope to secure the bags. When I asked him why, he told me that I would understand in a short time. Lesson four (why, at this rate, I am going to be a genius) the road will destroy everything that is not lashed down.

Four very tired Americans got into the Toyota double cab and headed for their home in the Zambian savanna. We were told that it would take us about two hours, and the road would be very rough. As we left the airport, we turned south on the main road. It was the main north/south route through Zambia, north to the border with Zaire and south to the border with Zimbabwe. Also, it was one of the few roads that was paved. As we headed south, the road was lined with people trying to get a ride. At first, we thought they were all waving at us. We knew the Zambians were very friendly people, and we thought this was our first exposure to their generous spirit. Actually, though, they were trying to wave down a ride. To get a ride you stood by the side of the road with an arm extended parallel. Then, starting at your shoulder, you would roll your arm up and down so it looked like a wave coming in from the lake. You did this until the wave reached your finger tips and then you did it all over again.

We left Lusaka and headed south. About forty-five minutes south we were stopped at the Kafue River. A military roadblock was at both ends of the bridge. Guards carrying AK-47's approached the truck and inquired as to who we were. As soon as they recognized the truck and our driver, they let us through. The roadblock had been there for some time. Rebels from Mozambique would enter Zambia using the Kafue River.

The country around us was beautiful. Gentle rolling hills with scattered Baobab trees and sweet smelling Jacaranda and Frangipani trees welcomed us to the bush. The ground looked like dry red clay, slightly rusty looking. I thought, "How in the world are we going to grow anything in soil like this?"

After about thirty minutes south of Kafue we turned down the road to our new home. Up to this point the road wasn't really that bad. There were a lot of potholes and bumps, but it wasn't too bad. We were used to traveling on rough roads. Whenever we went on vacation, we always took the girls down a road we called the "Bunny Trail." In northeast Michigan there are a lot of designated wilderness roads, and our Bunny Trail was one of them. It was eight miles of very rough gravel, at times a shale-topped bone jarring ride. As a young married family Donna and I would ride our bikes from town to my parents' home near Lake Huron. We would strap Marily in her child seat behind Donna and head down the Bunny Trail.

The Kata road was about twenty miles of the worst excuse for the term road that could be found. There were some stretches of good gravel where you could drive sixty or seventy mph if you wanted to. Those good sections of the road were probably less than a mile in length. After that, you would be driving on giant outcroppings of stone or miles of roadway consisting entirely of baseball-sized rocks. It was easy to see why everything needed to be tied down.

About forty-five minutes after turning down the road, we approached our new home. The land was beautiful. Picture perfect Tonga huts dotted the countryside. Men and women walked up and down the road. Some of the women were carrying large pails of water on their heads, going back to their village. As we got closer, we came to the area just outside the entrance to Kankata known as "The Grid." It was a gathering place. A few local people would sell bananas, tomatoes, or other vegetables if they had them. There were a couple of small shops as well. The shops were there to sell to the family members of hospital patients. In Zambia, the family was responsible for feeding their own family member in the hospital. For some it meant that they were away from their village for days or even weeks.

We crossed the cattle grid in the road and headed to our new home. About a quarter of a mile from the entrance was our house. The house was made of concrete block, and the floors were smooth- finished concrete. When the floors were just about dry, a red dye was spread over the concrete, a tint similar to that of the ground outside. The house was large by local standards. It had three bedrooms and a living and dining room open to each other. The kitchen was large with a pantry off to one side. Even out in the bush iron bars covered every window. They were to keep the thieves out.

We pulled into our drive, exhausted from two days of travel and stress. Our bodies were aching for some rest even though it was only mid-day. Before unloading everything we wanted to take a quick look around our new home. We went in the front door, and to our left was my office, to the right a set of doors that led into the house. Feeling a little bit of excitement, we wanted to look around; after all, this was going to be our home for at least the next four years. As Donna and I stepped into the kitchen, we had a welcome surprise waiting for us.

There was a spider as big as a baseball attached to the door of one of the cabinets. You know the kind of spiders that I am talking about. The big hairy ones, like the kind on the science fiction or Discovery channels. I thought Donna was going to blast off into orbit and never come down. I quickly grabbed the nearest weapon, a fly swatter, and went for him. Not only was he big, he was really fast. In an instant he was down the door and under the kick board of the cabinet. We would never see him again. And so, our first prayer uttered in Zambia was answered.

our first days

After looking around the house we unpacked our luggage. In a couple of hours we were going to have dinner with the medical director and his family. The next day, we would have dinner with the headmaster of the school and his family. During our first week we would have dinner at a different house each evening. This was planned to be a time of fellowship and getting to know each other. It also insured that the new family had at least one substantial meal each day. It would take a month before our garden would be able to produce, so the shared meal was important. The office in Lusaka made sure that each newly arriving family had some basic food items in their pantry and refrigerator. Items such as instant coffee, cabbage, tomatoes, and eggs were stocked for the newcomers. That first night we had a wonderful dinner. Hilary met a girl her age, and they became instant friends. After dinner and some friendly conversation we headed for home. A good night's sleep was what we needed. We got home and settled the girls in for the night. Wow, I thought! We are finally here. It just doesn't seem possible. A couple of days ago we were in Chicago; now I'm sitting in my living room in the bush.

It didn't take long for four exhausted bodies to fall asleep. Early the next morning, I woke up with two distinct thoughts in my head, the first one being, "What is that wonderful smell coming in through the window?" The second was, "What is that terrible noise that seems to rise and lower in pitch and volume?" The smell was the wonderful fragrance of the Jacaranda trees right across from our house. Their fragrance increased with the heat and intensity of the sun. The noise? It would become all too familiar. It was the sound of the mourning and wailing at the hospital morgue. It is hard to describe sounds and noises that come from deep within a grieving person. At times, the sounds were wailing; at other times they were a deep moaning or guttural groaning. The mourning would continue for hours or sometimes even days, until the body was taken away.

Donna and the girls spent the first day getting the house in order. It wouldn't take them very long since there wasn't yet much to put in order. We knew we had to wait four to six weeks for the containers to arrive. I walked up the road to the shop where I would spend most of my time. I wanted to get busy learning my various responsibilities. My job was to take care of the infrastructure of the entire compound and the fleet of vehicles. I would be responsible for water, electricity, and transportation management. I studied the detailed information sent to me prior to departure. The information detailed my three main responsibilities.

Years ago, an earthen dam was constructed to hold in the rain water. The lake would swell to about eighty acres during the rainy season. Our system of pumps and filters brought the water from the dam to each building on the compound. At the pump house the water was filtered through large sand filters and then pumped into a concrete storage container. Once a day when the filters were cleaned, the water was chlorinated. We also had a well, or borehole, as it was called here. The well provided water that would have to be carried to each house.

We were equipped with two large diesel-powered electrical generators. These provided electrical service to the community when the Zambian power was not operating. I was to run and maintain the system guaranteeing power to the hospital and school on a scheduled basis. I was told that the busiest time of the year would be during the rains when the generators would run for days at a time.

One of the things that I heard about prior to arriving was the devastating economy. The impact that it had on our ability to purchase supplies and parts was tremendous. In order to keep the fleet of vehicles operating we were in constant need of parts and supplies. Most of the replacement parts had to be ordered from Japan or South Africa. From the time the part was ordered to its arrival, its cost may have doubled or tripled. The mechanics that we had to work on the vehicles were self-taught, and that would prove to be expensive as well.

That night we had dinner with the headmaster of the secondary school. The school was the best in the country. Students came from all across Zambia to attend the school. Its reputation as a first-class educational institution was known in the highest levels of Zambian government and commerce. At the dinner with the headmaster we tried for the first time the main dish of the people, nshema. It was ground corn boiled until it was very thick, almost hard. You ate it with your hands. You would take a portion off of your plate and roll it between your fingers until you formed a small ball with it. If you had vegetables or a bit of meat, then you would eat it with the nshema. The taste seemed bland at first, kind of like overcooked corn mush or grits.

The third night, our dinner was at the house of the laboratory director and his family. They were from Canada and were delightful people. We arrived at their house and left our shoes on the porch, as was the custom. I left my ring of keys in my shoe as well because it was too big to keep in my pocket. We had a great dinner and made friends very quickly. Their son treated the girls like sisters, and they had a ball. It was late by the time we got ready to leave. It would be a long walk in the dark. When we got to the back door, we discovered that all of our shoes were gone. Someone stole our new shoes along with my keys. The funny part of this was I wore a size thirteen shoe, and they told me that nobody for miles around would have a foot that big. We laughed at the thought of my shoes being cut in half to make two pair. We had to walk home that night with nothing on our feet. The only thing that I could think of was stepping in bovine deposits as we stumbled home in the dark.

The week of our fellowship dinners went well. We were already sensing the tremendous friendliness of the Zambian people. One of the things that I was going to have to get used to, however, was the reaction of the children to me. At six feet, four inches tall and 240 pounds, they thought I was a giant. To put it mildly, the children from the villages were petrified of me. It bothered me for a while when they would cry and run away from me.

The following week we were supposed to enroll the girls in school. They would have to live in Lusaka and attend the International School. We went into Lusaka to register them and make their living arrangements. Marily would be in the upper levels of the Cambridge System. She would be attending school with the children of business owners and other foreign expatriates. The fees were very high, and our office in Chicago was gracious enough to cover the costs for us. Little Hilary, though, was not able to make the adjustment, and we decided to keep her with us. We would make do as best we could with her educational needs.

The first two weeks had passed. We had Marily in school. She was doing great, adjusting to the new educational system and living arrangements. She was living in a hostel run by an Australian couple who had two children of their own. She did have to learn about the meaning of words and how they are different in other cultures. For instance, she was told that she could not use the word "bangs" when referring to a girl's hair cut in that style. "Bangs" was a dirty word in Australia. The proper word was "fringe." She told me one day that she felt like telling the house mom that in America we didn't eat mashed potatoes with our hands as her son did. Yet, she told me she remembered her manners and kept her mouth shut. I think she liked school so much because she was surrounded by high achievers who were respectful and welcoming.

It was probably our second Sunday, and Marily was home for the weekend. She wanted to cook Sunday dinner. We had decided to have chicken, so Donna purchased a chicken that was freshly dressed. Marily took care of cooking the chicken, and with everything ready we sat down for dinner. As I cut the chicken, much to our surprise, the feet and head were inside the chicken. Needless to say, Marily didn't want to eat any chicken. To make it worse for Marily, Hilary took one of the chicken feet and chased her around the house. It was a weekend that we will never forget.

With Hilary's help Donna planted our garden. Once the garden began to produce, it would be a tremendous blessing. We had planted beans, peas, cabbage, carrots, eggplant, lettuce, radishes, and sweet corn. I was especially excited about the sweet corn. The local men that I talked with had never before eaten sweet corn. I was eager to let them try some of our Cream and Sugar variety. The corn they grew and ate was feed or field corn. At times they ate it on the cob roasted. Usually it was dried and then ground into a fine meal to make nshema, which we had eaten earlier, their most important staple food.

By this point, it was really setting in on us that we were living in Zambia. The Zambian people were so loving and friendly. They were a happy and joyful people. Their joy was wonderful to see. They were always smiling, and you could hear them singing any time of the day. The joy of God was very much alive in them, even in the midst of stark poverty. Some of our hardest adjusting was trying to deal with the poverty and its impact upon the children. Many of the children were dressed in rags that were hardly identifiable as pieces of clothing. It was even worse in the outlying areas away from the station and its limited benefits. The remote areas were a world of death and poverty that washed over multitudes of young and old alike.

One of our first Sunday nights we attended the chapel services for the nursing staff at the hospital. The service was held in their very small and hot chapel. I honestly did not know what to expect that night. So, I was thrilled to find that the service was filled with joyful, happy singing in Tonga, which I knew very little of. The joy and happiness of the nurses and others was awesome. One chorus, Tukalala Bosana, which we would come to love, actually got me on my feet trying to do their little dance to the beat of the drum. As I tried to turn around to the drum's lively beating, more than a couple of people laughed. This six-foot, four-inch white guy didn't have much rhythm.

placed into her hands

The wailing and moaning coming from the village traveled over the barren hills and few scrub trees to a village a couple of miles away. The noise means one thing; death had come upon the Kalumbu village. He knew his duty as a family member and walked to the village. Arriving at the village he found the women gathered around a small hut, built out of dried branches and held together with the rust-colored mud. Inside the hut his sister-in-law is dead. Placed on her stomach is a girl child, wrapped in her birth rag. The scene was evidence of the plague taking place across the land. A mother giving birth bleeds to death due to malnourishment and no care.

The tradition of his people dictate that the girl child is to be buried with the mother. It is taught that a child that can cause the death of a mother must possess a very powerful spirit and is to be buried. The young boys begin to dig the grave, not far from the edge of the village.

The man from the adjacent village is Dominic Kalumbu's brother, the girl child's uncle. As he listens to the wailing and talks with the older women he tells them he is troubled and fears they will have problems with the child. He tells them that a child that can cause the death of a mother could cause fears and problems as she will come and haunt the village. The chickens will not lay eggs and drought will cover the land. As his brother is away, the decision on what to do falls to him.

The ladies of the village tell him that the girl child will die within some hours as she is weak and there are no breasts that can give life to the child. He knows that this baby must possess a very powerful spirit. It would be best for the village if she would go away to die. The family in the village had wanted to follow tradition. The baby should be buried alive with her mother. She would die in a few moments as the earth that covers her mother covers her tiny, fragile body as well. It had been done that way for decades or even longer. The child is placed on the mother's body as the grave is dug. And then both are buried in the hope that their spirits do not linger and bring grief and troubles to the village.

With his brother gone for a while he knows what must be done. He tells the old women of the village what he is doing and why. They will not bury the girl child in the village. They all know that the baby wrapped in the birth rag is going to die. She weighs less than four pounds and is sickly looking. At least she will die someplace else. Picking her up from off her mother, he begins his walk north.

October is late spring in Zambia, and weeks can pass without a cloud in the sky. Night temperatures can easily drop to the low fifties. Mid-afternoon temperatures can easily rise above ninety to ninety-five degrees. The land has been plagued by droughts or very sporadic rains for the previous three years. Some areas may enjoy a normal rainfall, while areas not twenty miles away can suffer severely. The Chavuna-Chinjawa area is among the latter. Any water found is likely to be stagnant and used by animals.

As the infant's uncle walks on his way to Kankata, on the first day he passes a small clinic run by the Catholic Church. A couple of times he stops to drip some of the stagnant water into the baby's mouth. She is still alive, and he knows he must continue his walk. Like all of the Tonga people, he knows of Kankata. It was started by the white people sixty years before his days began. Now the hospital helps the Tonga people as well as people from all over Zambia.

The second day of his walk he enters the village area surrounding Kankata. Curious children and adults look to see what he is carrying in his arms. The mothers tell him that the baby is near death. Her skin is ashen, and death is just behind her. Knowing he must complete his walk, he heads to the hospital. If she had died on the way, he still would have brought her here, so when she died, she would be far away from the village.

He finds the entrance to the outpatient area and hands the baby to the white woman in the white uniform. He tells her, "She is baby Harriett. She was born two days ago and her mother is dead." As he finishes those words in broken English, he turns and heads back to Chavuna-Chinjawa. His task is done.

Donna is the white woman who holds on to the fragile life wrapped in the dirty and bloody rag. She contacts the doctor who is working the admission area, and he comes to perform an initial evaluation. While she is waiting for his arrival, she bathes and dresses the little one in a small gown.

The doctor's initial survey is grim. The infant is very near death. He tells Donna, "Put her into one of the small bassinets and let her go." But Donna is not about to let a little baby lie all alone waiting to die. She holds her for a few minutes and knows that it would be up to the Lord to keep her alive because the trauma could take her two-day-old life any moment.

Well, that little girl with the powerful spirit, survived the night and the early morning hours of the next day. That morning, Donna arrived with Hilary. Hilary wanted to help her mom with the new baby. One of the European doctors was performing a more thorough evaluation of the newly arrived baby. The results revealed that the little one was already battling intestinal parasites, most likely from the stagnant water she ingested the first day. Her mother's malnutrition had devastated her tiny body as well. Because of the malnutrition, the doctor told Donna, if the baby survived, she would be at risk of severe mental and physical difficulties. It may be more merciful for Donna to just let the infant slip away to a better and more secure world.

The doctors did not really understand how Donna felt about the spiritual power of love. She and Hilary were already demonstrating the power of love and human touch. On previous days Hilary would go to the hospital with her mother and help her with the babies. Hilary loved being with them and holding them. She was just like her mother. In the evening, they would tell me about their day and the babies. One evening, they were talking about Baby Irene. Baby Irene was in the last stages of AIDS. She would die any day now. They wanted to do something special for Irene. She had no family; no one ever came to hold her or talk with her except Donna and now Hilary. They wanted her to sense in her little heart that two people cared deeply for her. I thought it would be okay to let them bring Baby Irene home for the weekend. They would hold her and talk to her, and on Sunday we would take her to church. It was a very busy weekend for me, and on Sunday I finally got the chance to relax. Hilary used one of the dresses from a baby doll she brought with her to put on Irene. Irene was six months old, and she weighed no more than eight or nine pounds. As I looked at her for the first time, I was amazed. Her facial features looked old, and her hands were thin and weak. How could Donna and Hilary show such love and compassion for this little child? She would be dead in just a few days. How could they open themselves up for such pain?

We went to church that Sunday and then home for the afternoon. The next morning, Donna took Irene back to the hospital. My wife and daughter had taught me a very priceless truth: express love in understandable ways while you have the chance. On Tuesday morning, I was standing at the shop when I saw Donna coming up the road towards me. She was wiping some tears from her eyes. In a very tender voice she told me that Irene had just died and that she was holding her in her arms as God brought the ultimate healing to her little life. Her funeral was attended by only a couple of people besides Donna and Hilary. Hilary let her wear the little baby doll dress. The staff asked Donna to say a few words as they laid Irene in her grave. How is Donna going to be able to hold up as she loves these children and watches them die? It will be a hard time on her heart.

Well, Donna and Hilary decided to take extra time and care with the new baby who was just brought in. The malnutrition alone was enough to end the struggle of this new life. When you add the stress of the internal parasites, her survival would be nothing short of miraculous. She had survived the first couple of days, to almost everyone's surprise. Each day Donna and Hilary would bathe and care for the baby, who came to be known as Baby Harriett. A week passed, and the baby hung on. Two weeks passed, and she was still fighting for her life. The baby with the powerful spirit was surviving.

The hospital was without any formula, so we had to begin buying vitamin enriched formula from South Africa. It was expensive, and we had to travel into the Capitol to buy it at the government-run shop. We had to pay with American funds, so we used the small amount of money that we had. At this point, we decided that whatever the cost was we were going to buy what was needed. The formula seemed to be helping, and soon her second month at the hospital had arrived.

Near the end of November, some disturbing things began taking place with the orphan babies. In the span of one week three of the little babies died. The nursing staff did not know why. The doctors attributed the deaths to influenza. There were only two little ones surviving in the nursery. After talking it over with the nursing staff, the Principal Nursing Officer brought baby Harriett to our house. Donna told me about the other babies dying, and we agreed to take care of her in our home, thinking it might be safer than the nursery.

a mother's heart
and the hand of God

$$\diagup\!\!\!\diagdown\diagup\!\!\!\diagdown\diagup\!\!\!\diagdown$$

*F*rom our very first days in Zambia the rainy season was an important topic and concern. When will it begin? How much rain will there be? How long will the rains last? All of this was so different for me. Back in Michigan precipitation came year-round. But in Zambia rainfall took place from December through March or early April. The other months of the year the sun would shine in a cloudless sky for days, or even weeks.

According to the local people the rains were coming late. I thought that I was ready for the rains to begin. I knew the electrical and water systems pretty well. We had a good supply of fuel for the generators. One generator was dedicated to supply the hospital with power, and the other would be used to supply the school and, on a rotating basis, the residences.

The rainy season also disrupted the supply of clean water. The filtration system could only be used sparingly when there was no

Zambian power. The water needed to be pumped about a quarter of a mile from the dam to the pump house. At the pump house the water was filtered and then chlorinated before going into the storage tank. During the rains the water supply to the houses was cut off. Everybody knew that when it started to sprinkle, you filled up your bathtub, sink, and every bucket and pan you could find.

The first rains began right around Christmas. It was hard getting used to December temperatures and humidity levels, both of which were almost always at one hundred. Within days the rain pattern took shape. The cloud cover would move from the south and grow turbulent. It would begin to rain in the middle to late afternoon and rain into the night. During some evenings and nights a storm would bring in the most spectacular displays of lightning I had ever seen. At times it seemed like the horizontal streaks could last five or ten seconds. It was awesome to watch the displays of blues, whites, and yellows as they streaked across the night sky.

Since the first of December Donna had been taking care of baby Harriett in our home. She was so small. Her eyes seemed to bulge, and she wasn't very responsive. With the onset of the rains I was very busy. I didn't have much time to be home. I was in and out at lunch and had dinner when I could. During this entire time Donna never complained or was upset about how hard life was. She made diapers out of old bath or hand towels. She cut down t-shirts to make sleepers for baby Harriett. Whatever was needed for the baby Donna found a way to provide.

The rains also provided a couple of really fascinating displays of nature. During one of the rains I was on my way to the pump house. This time, when I walked in, I found one of the walls covered with black ants. The wall behind the filters was covered with thousands of ants about a half inch in length. The eight foot by twenty foot wall looked like one black mass. On the floor in front of me was a large dead rat. It was lying in the drain trough just in front of the tanks. As if given some silent command, the ants began moving down the wall and covering the floor. By this time I was standing on a piece of piping that was coming out of the concrete floor. As I watched, the ants, seemingly thousands, moved into the trench and covered the rat. And then the rat began to move. The mass of ants was moving the rat down the trough. The swarm steadily maneuvered the rat down the trough and out the hole in the wall. I had just witnessed the most incredible display of teamwork I had ever seen. It probably took that synergistic army only five minutes to rid the building of the rat.

On another occasion Hilary and I were attacked by biting red ants. She had been helping me with the water system one evening, and as we headed for home, the road was like a flowing stream. We noticed that the water on the road looked like it was peppered with thousands of dots. When we got out of the truck to look, hundreds of red ants swarmed up our legs. In an instant I got Hilary into the truck, and I sped towards the house. In a matter of seconds my truck was in the driveway. Before we even hit the living room door, we were peeling off our clothes. Hilary made it to the bathroom and finished stripping. I thought that I had all of the biting red devils off of me until the back of my knee felt like a red hot poker was sticking it.

This first rainy season brought a lot of new and different experiences for us. It was difficult to have Marily in Lusaka. When the rains were heavy, you couldn't drive the Kata road. Marily would have to spend many of her weekends in Lusaka. We were a very close family, and it was hard on all of us to have her so far away. We looked forward to her weekends with us. It seemed that she missed so much of what was happening. Of necessity at this point her contact with the baby was pretty limited.

Near the end of the rainy season Donna's heart was to face its gravest test. It had been raining for the entire day and night, so I didn't have much time at home. I finally made it home in the middle of the night to find Donna sleeping in the chair holding onto baby Harriett. When I woke up Donna, she immediately moved the little life out of the cradle of her arm so she could see her face. As she moved her, baby Harriett stirred. With tears streaming down her face she said, "Thank you, Jesus. She is alive." During the night she began having convulsions. In a short time they were almost constant. When one convulsion ended, within moments another began. Donna got in touch with her friend, the doctor from the Netherlands. The doctor told Donna to hold her and keep her comfortable because she probably wouldn't survive the night. Convulsion after convulsion shook the fragile little body. That night Donna told me that she gave the precious little one back to God. After crying and praying, Donna fell asleep, exhausted and not knowing if the morning would bring her, her own time of mourning.

That rainy night in the Zambian bush a mother's heart moved the Hand of God. Nothing less than a miracle began to unfold. A fragile suffering child survived, and a mother became connected in her soul with that fragile life. The bond between Donna and her heart-adopted child was forged that night. It was at this point in Baby Harriet's survival and Donna's dedication that I knew in my heart we must try to adopt her. Her struggle for life and her determination had left an imprint upon our hearts and spirits. We knew that we wanted to be with her every day of her life, no matter how long or short it was.

As a family we began talking about wanting to adopt our angel. One of the first decisions that we needed to make was to give our girl a beautiful name. We decided to think about her name for a few days and then talk again. Within a couple of days Donna told us that she knew the perfect name. We would name her Ana Syoma. Ana means "God's gift," and Syoma is a Tonga word meaning, "that which we hope for." Her name was perfect; she was God's Gift of Hope, to us and many others. Yet, little did we know how much she would prove to be our Gift of Hope over and over again.

a weekend in paradise

With the rains finally over, I was exhausted. I was glad to see them end, and I enjoyed the cloudless sky with new appreciation. The task of keeping everything running wore me out. We had been working hard for six months, and now it was our chance to get away for a weekend with the girls.

We were going to Kariba, Zimbabwe. A family from the states operated a retreat called, Most High. We had heard a lot about the place, and we were really looking forward to going. The retreat had a nice swimming pool and the food was supposed to be fabulous. I had lost sixty pounds in the six months since arriving. The secret to my weight loss was the combination of walking about ten miles a day and eating fresh vegetables and fruit from the garden. These past six months we ate very little meat and some poultry. As a reward for my self-denial, I now intended to devastate their buffet.

With Ana's travel document and our passports in hand, we were ready to go. The girls were so excited. We had heard about the elephants and other wildlife we would see. So we packed the back of the truck and headed off to Kariba. With a cap on the back of the truck and a foam mattress on the truck bed, the girls were very comfortable. The ride would take a couple of hours. Our friends warned us to keep our windows closed after we crossed into Zimbabwe. It seemed that the baboons liked to get into cars. Once inside, it was very hard to get them out, and they would tear apart the inside of your car.

We arrived at the border crossing and really didn't know what to expect. After parking the truck, all five of us went into the office. The office was long and narrow. The immigration officer was seated at a very small desk at the end of the room. The desk looked like an old table with a single drawer. We had our passports, immunization records, and Ana's travel document all ready for his inspection. After some pleasant remarks the officer asked us where we were going and for how long. I told him we were going to Most High for the weekend. He wished us a nice weekend and prepared to stamp our papers. With our passports and other documents arranged on his desk, he took his stamp and stamp pad out of the drawer. Almost in slow motion he set the pad in front. Then, he placed the stamp, with very precise movements, next to the pad. His every move seemed very precise and timed. He opened the first passport to the pages reserved for immigration stamps, deliberately holding the passport open with his left hand. He picked up the stamp and gently rolled it over the pad. The stamp was flat, and he took care to makes sure there was plenty of ink on it. With the well-inked stamp he took careful aim and slammed the stamp down on the passport. The sound rang out in the little room, a mixture of the smacking on paper and the thud on wood. He repeated this precise procedure for the passports and Ana's travel document. It was pretty hard to keep a straight face; I wanted to laugh.

After leaving the office and getting back into the truck, I thought about the whole episode. I came to the realization that the job the immigration officer had made him feel important, just as it had with the customs official at the airport long before. First, he had a job; most Zambians lived by subsistence farming. Second, it was his responsibility to make sure all travelers had the proper documents. I guess his dramatic stamping of the documents was his way to remind himself and others of the importance of his job.

We crossed into Kariba on the roadway on top of the dam. Lake Kariba spreads out for miles on our right side of the road. Kariba is one of the largest man-made lakes on the African continent. The lake is teeming with wildlife. The elephants and deer species come to it every day for their water. The giant hippos are always visible swimming about near the shore. The lake's fishery is a big economic boost to the area. Fishermen on both sides of the lake go out at night and net the plentiful Kapenta fish, a fish about as small as a minnow. After a night of fishing, the catch is spread out on nets about four feet off the ground. The fish are kept out in the sun until they dry. They are eaten by themselves or added to the ground corn dish.

The small town of Kariba sits on top of a hill overlooking the lake, across which the Zambian hillside is clearly visible. Kariba has a slightly western culture. There is a small business area with some nice shops and an ice cream stand. It is a very clean town, and the people are exceptionally friendly. As I drove up to the retreat, a group of women were sitting near a rock wall directly across from us. Donna noticed they had beautiful lace work on display. Donna and Hilary decided that as soon as we got settled, they were going to take a look.

At the retreat we had two rooms. One room was for Marily and Hilary, and another room for Donna, Ana, and myself. We had a bassinet put into our room for Ana. By western standards the rooms were very modest. By Zimbabwe standards they were nice. But by Zambian standards they were luxurious. As soon as we settled in, Donna and Hilary headed across the road. The ladies greeted them and told Donna how beautiful Hilary's long blond hair was. The women had made beautiful white doilies and tablecloths. They were all laid out for people to look at. Donna fell in love with a beautiful white tablecloth. After some serious negotiations Donna had her tablecloth. In the meantime, Hilary had found a small white doily and asked if one of the ladies could turn the doily into a little hat for Ana. In a matter of minutes the doily was transformed, and Ana was wearing her new hat.

I wanted to go swimming. It was hot outside, and the pool was calling my name. After taking baths all rainy season in red water, the pool looked really nice. We got ready to go, and Donna had found a tiny two-piece suit for Ana. It was red with white stripes. At six months old she was still very tiny. I picked her up and carried her down to the pool. I would begin with Ana just as I did with the other girls. I held them in my arms and bobbed up and down in the water. First, I only got their feet wet, and then little by little the rest of their body. As long as I held them tight, they knew they were safe. I would do the same with Ana. She had never been in a pool. Holding her in my arms, I got her feet wet. She started to shiver and was frightened. Her lip began to quiver, and she was about to cry.

Holding on to Ana, I told her, "Don't be afraid. Daddy will hold you tight." In that swimming pool in Kariba I voiced what my heart had felt for a long time. I told that innocent struggling life that I was her daddy. I knew that I loved her the very first time I held her tiny body in one of my hands. How could any human being not love and cherish such a beautiful little child. I knew that I loved her, yet I was uncertain how much pain we could endure if she died. I guess that I decided that any pain would be worth it, and I would be her dad. We continued to play for a while. Then Donna took her and wrapped her up, and the two of them took a nap in the warm sun. Again, I decided that I would do whatever was needed to help her become a part of our family.

Our time at Most High was fabulous. We had so much fun together. We went out in the evening looking for wild game. Each evening we would see four or five species of deer. Their grace and speed were amazing to watch. One evening as we were heading back, a female lion ran across the road in front of us. By far, the most fun we had was with the elephants. Each evening they would come into town and head for the swimming pools. About a hundred yards from the pool at Most High was a municipal pool. At night the elephants would come into town and go to the pools to drink and eat the leaves off the banana trees. As one might guess, the problem with the thirsty pachyderms is what they left behind after their nightly visits. Any animal left-behinds in the states can't even begin to compare to an elephants'. So, each evening when the elephants showed up, we would walk to within fifty feet or so and holler and make a lot of noise, trying to get them to leave. Elephants, besides having a great memory, are extremely stubborn creatures. Our host at the retreat center assured us that we would be safe. Safe that is, unless one of the big brutes flared out his ears and trumpeted. If that were to happen, then one had better be able to sprout wings or be really prayed up.

Our wonderful weekend came to a close far too soon. Sunday evening we headed back to Zambia. We had been able to swim, drink a Coke, eat fabulous meals, and enjoy the wildlife. It was a great time.

But, a little over a week after our return, I would begin to pay dearly for my weekend. On the Saturday night of our weekend we got ready to go to bed. We didn't really like sleeping with the mossy net over us, so we never used them. Before going to bed I would look around the room to make sure there were no unwanted visitors. Spiders, really ugly ones, and geckos were the usual visitors. In their haste to retreat, the geckos would usually leave part of themselves behind, their tail. And, there were basically two kinds of spiders, the friendly and the other kind. Friendly spiders were flat and usually lived behind the pictures on the wall. They were friendly because they ate the mosquitoes. Well, that night there were no spiders or geckos to dispatch to the other world. But there was one mosquito to take care of. Yet, try as hard as I did, I could not kill that lousy bug. After a few minutes of frustrating attempts I decided that one lousy mosquito really couldn't hurt anything. I was wrong!

Sometime during that night that single, solitary, parasite laden, I-don't-know-why-God-created-them, mosquito, bit me. That next week I woke up with the worst headache I had ever had. The pain in my head made me think that my cranium was going to blow any moment. In a couple of hours diarrhea was added to the drums pounding in my head. It took me some time to make my way up to the hospital. Tests soon revealed what everybody was already telling me: malaria. The incubation period is around seven to ten days. And, as near as I could figure it, the intruder at Most High was the culprit.

I found myself in a hospital room about ten-by-ten. The room, painted an off-white had one window and no curtains. The bed I was on seemed left over from the Mayflower. I could hardly fit on it, and the springs felt like they were being grafted to my underside. But my room was much better than being in one of the wards. I just had to get used to the bed and the cockroaches that ran all over everything. Those critters couldn't even be slowed down. It was like they were running to find all of their little creepy friends to come and see the big white man in the tiny bed. I imagined them pointing their ugly front legs at me and laughing. After a few days I responded to my medication and began to feel better. A good friend even brought me a cold Coke, a rare treat most days. I was glad the illness didn't progress to cerebral malaria. From the beginning of the rainy season the wailing at the morgue never ended because of malaria. As a young child I remember my father telling us stories about World War II and how he was infected with cerebral malaria. I didn't want to repeat his experience.

Just a few days later, Hilary came down with malaria as well. The headache and accompanying symptoms hit her real hard. I knew how she was feeling. It was very hard for me seeing her in the hospital so sick. I honestly had never thought about my children getting ill. Would my calling to the mission field endanger my children? Did I have the right to do that? It was so easy out in the bush for bad things to happen. The spiders could bite; there were all kinds of very dangerous snakes as well. Did I really know what I was getting my family into? I came to realize that if God called me, and ultimately Donna and our family, then He would be taking care of us. Hilary had a lot of visitors, and the staff took wonderful care of her. In a little over a week she was able to come home. It would still take a couple of weeks for her to gain her strength back. Malaria leaves one very weak for quite a while.

an unexpected visit

With the rainy season behind me, I had survived my first onslaught of torrential rain and working around the clock. All around us the vegetation had turned a wonderful lush green. The sun was ripening the priceless gardens. Not far from the front of our house was a lemon tree. The tree looked like it was filled with bright yellow tennis balls. I picked lemons, and Donna boiled the juice and made lemonade. It was better than any I had ever tasted before. Our whole garden was producing for us. Initially we had some radishes and carrots. A short time later the cabbage ripened. With the blessing of the rains we had beans, peas, cabbage, sweet corn, eggplant, and strawberries.

We had decided that when the rains were over, we wanted to raise a pig. So, we got one from the secondary school. They raised their own pigs, cattle, and chickens. What they didn't use in the school cafeteria was sold. We named our pig, "Max," for I wanted to get the maximum benefit from him. The pig spent his lazy days eating pig-weed and basking in the sun. Now Max was one smart porker. He could recognize the sound of my truck coming down the road. Each evening I would come home with food for him. Usually, it was left over nshema from the nursing school. Donna told me that Max would begin squealing as soon as he heard my truck. When I would pull into the driveway, Max would be standing with his front hooves on the top rail of his fence. His little corkscrew pigtail spinning in circles, and he squealed until I dumped his food into the pan. Our friends told us not to name him since it would be too difficult to part with him when the time came. Well, the thought of ham, pork chops, and bacon seemed more powerful than saying goodbye to a pig. It was food over sentiment.

It was on one of those nice sunny days that we got an unexpected visit. I was home for lunch, when someone began knocking at the front door. The man standing at the door told me he was Dominic Kalumbu, the father to the baby we had. I invited him in and called Donna to come into the living room. He told us that he came looking for the child's grave. The nurses told him that the baby was alive and that we were caring for her. They told him how to find our house as well. I have to say I was feeling very uneasy. What did he want? Would he take her away from us? Questions filled my anxious mind.

Donna and I sat down, and Dominic sat on a chair in front of us. We told him how the baby was doing and he said that he wanted to see her. Donna went into our bedroom and brought her out. She was about seven months old, and she was just beginning to gain strength. He asked if he could hold her, and Donna placed her in his arms. I didn't like the way I was feeling. I was feeling anxious and nervous. After my time with Ana in the pool in Kariba, she owned my heart. I wanted to be her father. Here in my living room was her real father. What were his intentions? If he wanted to take her back, there was nothing we could do to stop him. We knew if she went back in her condition, she would be dead within weeks. One of the most important reasons she was doing better was the formula we had been fortunate to buy.

After he held her for a few minutes, he gave her back to Donna. He thanked us for taking such good care of her. We told him she was a wonderful little girl and a gift from God. Just before he left, he told us that he would like us to care of her until she turned one, and then he would take her back to the village. After telling us that, he said goodbye and began his walk back. That meant that we would only have her for four or five more months.

We thought, how can we do this? We already love her as our own flesh and blood. Now we feel that if we send her back we would be signing her death sentence. We were living in a land that is as destitute as depicted on the mission posters back in the states. The ground in the valleys is parched and dead. Little children sit on the ground covered with dirt and flies. Families struggle to live on what the ground could produce for them. Every day little children die of malnutrition and other childhood illnesses. Illnesses long eradicated in the states still kill thousands of infants in Africa.

If we could only have our Ana until she was one, then God would have to help us deal with the pain. We prayed that the Lord would give us grace and, if possible, help us keep Ana, our Gift of Hope.

Later that day, we had to tell Hilary about the visit. Her heart was broken at the thought of sending her little Ana back to the village. She and Donna cried for a while. We told her to pray for the right thing to happen. During all of this, of course, Marily was in school. We were only able to tell her what was happening when she was fortunate enough to come home for the weekend. It would be difficult for Marily as well. Our girls are such loving and caring young people. Even though Marily didn't have as much contact with our little angel, she loved her as much as we did. At times I thought it might be a blessing for Marily to miss some of the stress we lived under. At least she had clean water and electricity every day.

Thoughts about the dangers of living in the bush crept in again. It didn't help any when just a couple of weeks before this I had an AK47 pointed towards my head. We were on our way to the capital of Zimbabwe for a dental appointment for Marily. It was hard to believe that in the entire country of Zambia there wasn't an orthodontist who could help Marily with her braces. So we had to take her to Zimbabwe for her adjustments.

On one trip we took a fellow missionary with us. She had been in the country for a long time. She had spent many years in Zimbabwe. In fact, she was living in Zimbabwe when the revolution took place. She told us about two of her friends who were killed by machine gun fire. They were in a vehicle plainly marked with the mission's logo. As they passed through a checkpoint, a guard, seemingly without reason, shot them.

Well, on this trip to Zimbabwe we approached a checkpoint in a small town, and I began to slow down. It was unusual because we had never encountered a checkpoint here before.

I brought the truck to a stop and rolled down my window about halfway. Our passenger friend whispered to me to lock my door. As the armed soldier approached, I pushed down the lock with my elbow. The soldier asked where we were going, and as he asked, the unmistakable smell of home-brewed alcohol filled the cab. He began to question us about why we had to travel and what the real nature of our travel was. He moved to the back of the truck and looked in where the girls were. As he moved to the back, our passenger told me in a very hushed voice to not get out of the truck, for any reason.

He came back to my side and tipped the muzzle of his weapon towards me. "Who is the girl child in the back?" he asked me. I told him that she was an orphan that we were taking care of. Seeming to be satisfied, and to all of our great relief, he waved me on.

our first visit to chavuna- chinjawa

﹀﹀﹀

hen we were in Kariba, Donna and I had talked a little about trying to adopt Ana. Now with what we were bearing in our hearts, it was time to talk about it as a family. We all agreed that Ana was such a part of us that we wanted her as part of our family. We knew that we really needed to visit her family. If the extended family knew how much we loved her, then maybe we could have more time with her.

A couple of weeks passed, and we made plans to go out to Ana's village for the first time. I had to arrange for somebody to cover my duties because it would take us all day to travel there and back. After talking to a couple of the men in the shop, we felt we could find the village.

We left very early in the morning. We brought enough water for Ana's formula and for us to drink. We were told to never drink water from a village area or from the local streams. Our systems could never handle the invisible invaders potentially living in the water.

We headed to Mazabuka and from there took a small two-track road for an hour or so. Unexpectedly, the road ended at some very large boulders. I didn't remember the men telling me about this. Now what were we going to do? We talked about turning around and going back home. We would have to try again using a different route. As we were trying to decide what to do, we saw a young man walking toward us from across a field. As he approached, we greeted him, and like all of the young Tonga men he was very friendly and polite. His English was excellent. After explaining to him what we wanted to do he told us that he would take us there. We would have to leave the truck and walk to the village. I asked him how far it was, and he told me that it would only take a short time. He knew the village, and he knew Ana's father. He had heard about us, the Maguah, who were taking care of the little Tonga girl.

With Ana wrapped in a chitangi on Donna's back, we headed off down a trail. Soon we were past the field of boulders and headed for what looked like gentle rolling hills. Looks are deceiving, and the gentle hills turned into some pretty steep grades. The air temperatures were rising, and so were ours. As we walked, I noticed the young man would look into the trees as we passed by. After an hour we stopped for a rest. I asked him why he was looking in the trees all of the time. He told us that some nasty snakes liked to hide in the trees. Thank you, Lord, for our guide!

After about a three-hour walk we arrived at the village. It sat atop a small rise, and there were only three or four small, scrubby trees in the area. The ground was very dry, even after the rains. The little children must have seen us coming because they were hollering and yelling in excitement. When we entered the village, there were about twenty people coming to meet us. The scene could have easily come from a National Geographic magazine. The little children were barely clothed, and what they were wearing was not much better than rags. The older women of the village wore their chitangi and a shirt.

We took special care to greet everybody in the proper way. First, I greeted each adult, beginning with the oldest. Then, I greeted the children, beginning with the oldest. When I was done, Donna greeted them the same way. The children seemed fascinated by us. They pointed and giggled as they talked with each other. I could imagine what they were saying as they looked at the big white man with his little wife. We were introduced to Ana's half-brother and half-sister. They were more than a year older then Ana. They were not much taller than she was. Her half-brother was almost blind because of measles. Her half-sister had lost almost all of her hair from malnutrition.

After the greetings we went into a smaller hut to talk. The hut was about fifteen feet in circumference. As we talked about Ana, Dominic would translate for us because the older women did not understand English. We wanted them to see Ana and how much we loved and cared for her. As this was our first visit, I didn't know what to expect, nor did I want to stay too long. Before we left, we gathered all of the family together and took some photographs. We promised to bring some back with us the next time we came.

As we prepared to leave, we were asked to visit another village. The village of Ana's grandfather was just a short distance from there. We agreed, and it was just a short walk. After her grandfather greeted us, we talked for a few minutes. He was very proud to hold Ana and have his picture taken with her. With the day running short, we knew we needed to head back to the truck. Our young guide led us back, and we thanked him for his wonderful help to us.

We were off for home. This entire day was going to take some time to sink into me. Ana's village was poor beyond belief. The children ate what was available. They were so sickly looking it broke our hearts. The land was so dry that the little bit of corn that was planted was almost dead. It wasn't like these people could just pack up and move. They couldn't move, this was their home. This was the land given to them by the headman. This land was their only home, where they lived, gave birth, and died. Even if they could move, how would they? Where would they go? They couldn't walk fifty or a hundred miles to find land where the rains were plentiful. It was not an option, so they did the best they could. Some lived, and some died. It was that simple in this land.

When we arrived home, we told Hilary about the village. We told her about Ana's half-brother and half-sister and how sick they were. We told her that the next time we were able to go out to the village we would take her with us. But we would have to find a better route, so we wouldn't have to walk as far. And the next time we went, we would take along a ninety-kilogram bag of meal for the family. I thought that a bag of that size should last them for about a month.

We decided to go the following month if we could work out the details. This wasn't as easy as traveling back home. The price of fuel was very high, the equivalent of about five dollars per gallon. And I had to be sure that all of my responsibilities for the day were covered.

A little over one month later, we were able to travel to the village again. This trip was going to be a lot easier. One of our friends was going with us. He said he knew a route that would take us right to the village. We loaded the truck early in the morning with our water and food supplies for the family. Hilary was very excited about the trip. She was turning into quite a little adventurer. She loved living in the bush and all the adventure she could have. We thought the trip would take us a couple of hours.

In a little over two hours we approached the village. And yes, sure enough, I was able to drive right up to it. Our route was so much easier. I had taken a familiar road and then a short jog over open country. The little children were already waiting; they heard the truck coming from a long way off. A soon as they recognized us, they were running alongside and waving. We parked and got out. The older women were happy to see Donna and Ana. After greeting everyone in the proper way, we sat down outside and talked. Donna told them how Ana was doing, that she was getting stronger every day. A short time later our friend told us the family members were commenting in Tonga about how wonderful the infant was looking.

As we sat there and talked, a really remarkable thing happened. The children would sneak up behind Hilary and touch her hair. Then they would giggle and run away. Hilary had beautiful long blond hair. The children had never seen soft blond hair before. Donna noticed what they were doing and had them sit beside Hilary. As they sat beside Hilary, they would touch and run their fingers through her soft hair. It didn't bother Hilary when she understood why they wanted to touch her hair.

Prior to this trip, we decided that we were going to begin talking about our wanting to adopt Ana. I knew that it would take a long time, and it would be a difficult decision. I also knew that we needed to begin doing so on this trip. It was hard to know when we would be able to come out again. So, as we talked, I brought up the subject of us wanting to raise Ana as our own child. As usual, our friend would interpret for us. I told him that I wanted to know what was said and the feeling behind their words. When I used the word adoption, the family seemed confused. They had never heard the word before and had no idea what it meant. Donna and I both explained how much we loved Ana and wanted her to grow strong and be healthy, and that we wanted her to become one of our children. We continued the conversation for just a few more minutes and then changed the subject. I knew that this was something that Dominic was going to have to think about for a long time. He would discuss it with all of the elders in his village, as well as with Ana's grandfather in the neighboring village.

We left the family with the ground meal and sensed that we had a very good visit. Just before we departed, we told Dominic that we would try to come back in a couple of months. He thanked us for the meal and told us that he would think about what we discussed. Our friend told us about the woman's conversation and how they were remarking back and forth about how much we cared for Ana. One of the eldest women told Dominic that if Ana came back to the village, she would become like the other children, or die. Donna and I knew that it was going to take time and prayer for things to work out. Deep inside, we trusted that God brought Ana to us for a reason. If there was no purpose for her life, then why did she survive the journey and those long struggling nights?

life in the city

∧∧∧

ust a few weeks after our first visit to Ana's village, I was informed I was being transferred to the regional office in Lusaka. I was now responsible for all of the property and building projects in Zambia and Malawi. This news filled me with a lot of different emotions and thoughts. On the plus side, we were together as a family because we would be living in the same flat that Marily had been in for the previous year. The family who had been living there was returning home, and I was taking over his responsibilities.

But as we already knew, life in the city would very different from our quiet life in the bush. We had to leave a lot of friends behind, and that was difficult. My new responsibilities would be challenging. The churches in Zambia were growing, and there were a lot of building projects going on. I was really looking forward to the traveling that I would get to do as I visited the rural areas that were building their churches.

To say that life in Lusaka was different is an understatement in the extreme. In the bush, life was pretty relaxed and relatively safe. But living in Lusaka was neither relaxed nor safe. Our apartment was on the compound with the administrative offices. Besides our main office building, there were six or seven more buildings on the compound. The entire compound was surrounded by a concrete block wall about twelve feet high. The top of the wall was covered with broken glass protruding out of the concrete. Above that, razor wire was strung along the entire perimeter. The only way into the compound was through the entrance gate. The gate was sheet steel with observation slots at about eye level. The gate was as tall as the walls, and at the top of the gate, pointed steel spikes had been welded every two or three inches. The gate was controlled every hour of every day of the year. The compound was a fortress.

Our apartment had three bedrooms, a living room, kitchen and dining room. One of the bedrooms would be used if other children of missionaries needed to live in the capital, as had happened with Marily. We had plenty of room, and the furnishings were more than adequate for our needs. It was going to be so nice being together. Ana was almost ten months old at this point, and her health continued to improve. As Ana grew stronger, we thanked God, yet in the back of our mind the thoughts of having to give her up was always there. Some people might have accused me of not having enough faith. It wasn't my faith that was weak, it was my ability to accept God's will if it meant Ana would be going back to the village. Still very much aware of the severe deprivation of her first days of life, we were still quite concerned about her physical development. We noticed that even as Ana generally grew stronger, her legs seemed to be malformed. They were as bowed as a pretzel. We knew it was from the malnutrition and could be a long-term problem. We believed her best hopes for optimal development would be best realized if she could remain a member of our family.

One of the benefits of living in the city was getting together with other Americans and westerners. Frequently, we would get together for coffee and the occasional holiday parties that we could go to. Usually, part of the time was spent talking about life in the city and what was happening. Americans and all westerners were the targets of robbers and pickpockets. Most westerners lived in homes protected as our compound was.

It was at one of our coffee talks that I first heard about "The Flying Squad." The Flying Squad was a security rapid response team in the city. It was made up of recruits with police and military background. Most of the members were not Zambians. They were in contact with police, businesses, and westerners living in the city. They communicated by radio around the clock. Their job was to get to the scene of a robbery or break-in as fast as possible, that is how they got their name, Flying Squad. When they arrived on the scene of a robbery they took whatever steps were required to stop it. Some robbers were caught and turned over to the police. Others couldn't be turned over to the police; they were taken to the morgue.

One very shocking event took place not even a hundred yards from our apartment. One night at two in the morning an explosion knocked me out of bed. I have always been a pretty light sleeper so I was on my feet in a second and heading out the door to the front gate. When I got to the gate, one of our guards was standing in the road. As I approached the guard, a Canadian friend was coming through the gate as well. In a moment we could tell what took place. Evidently, robbers were trying to break into an international radio communications company. They had intended to blow the door off using explosives. Most doors were covered with burglar bars. In this case the main door was protected with an outside door of sheet steel. The door was locked in two places, and the locks were protected with a section of four-inch steel pipe. A section of the pipe, about four to six inches long, was welded over the joining part of the hasp for the lock. To unlock it, one had to get the key into the pipe and into the lock. The pipe system was designed to keep people from using bolt cutters or other tools to cut the locks off.

Apparently, the bandits thought that they could blow the locks off using dynamite. They placed dynamite at each lock and then placed a heavy sheet of plywood against the outside of the door. They filled the space between the plywood and the lock with concrete. The concrete was intended to force the explosion inward, blowing off the locks and the door. To hold the force of the explosion in, they attempted to secure the plywood to the door by wiring it tight against the door using the burglar bars themselves. It didn't work, the explosion disintegrated the plywood. One of the sections of pipe that secured the lock was found in our compound about 200 yards from the radio shop. The shocked and empty- handed robbers quickly left. The steel door was badly mangled but still on its hinges.

Our second Christmas in Zambia was fast approaching. It was during the holidays that we missed being home the most. We had been so family-oriented all of our married life; it was hard being away from family members. This Christmas, like our first, would prove to be quite different.

On Christmas Day it was hot, and we were going to have a cookout with some friends. Ana got a Radio Flyer wagon for Christmas. It was sent months before and arrived in time for me to put it together. Marily and Hilary each received some Zambian silver jewelry and a couple of clothing items.

The day after Christmas we decided to take a walk downtown and pull Ana in her new wagon. We were heading for the duty-free shop, which was almost at the far end of the downtown business section. I was having fun pulling Ana in her wagon. She would giggle and laugh whenever I went a little fast or went over a bump. At each intersection I would take Ana out of the wagon and carry her across the street. The reason was simple: pedestrians never had the right of way. It wasn't the law that made it that way; it was the absolutely crazy drivers. It was every person for oneself when walking anywhere.

I still have a very vivid memory of the callousness and disregard for life that some people had. One day, as I was traveling on the south end of town, I watched as a little girl in her green and white school uniform, was hit by a bus, her body was catapulted through the air like a rag doll. I turned around as quickly as I could in the middle of the road and went back to the scene. When I got there, the bus driver was helping a taxi cab driver put the little girl in the back seat of his taxi. As I walked to the taxi, the driver closed the door and told me he was going to take the girl to the hospital as fast as he could. As the taxi pulled away, I looked in and saw her twisted body. She didn't look alive. I doubted that any child could survive that impact. Later that day as I told the story to a good friend, he told me that she probably never made it to the hospital, and they would probably find her body in a couple of days out in a field.

As we were crossing one intersection with Ana, a group of young men tried to pick my pocket. The usual scenario worked like this. The group would pick a target and then split up. One group of men would walk towards the target, and the second group would come behind the target. One of the men in the approaching group would bump into the target. When he did, the men in the back would go for the target's wallet or belly bag or backpack.

Well, as we were walking down the street, I was the target. This time as we crossed the intersection, I was carrying Ana in one arm and pulling the wagon with the other. In the intersection one of the men ran into the front of me. When he did, I felt the man in the back go for my wallet. It was too bad for him because I learned to carry my wallet in my front pocket. I pushed him out of the way, and when they realized they were empty-handed they left. I was so mad I wanted to spit. Here we were, walking as a family, and some dumb thugs wanted to rob us.

We continued on and did some shopping at the duty-free shop. As we began heading back home, the same gang was coming toward us again. Well, I guess some people are slow learners. They thought we wouldn't notice that they had changed shirts. As they approached us, the same thing happened. This time I was ready for them. When the one in the front hit me, the one in the back went for the bags I was carrying. Boy, were they in for a big surprise. I grabbed the front guy by the front of his shirt and lifted him off the ground. I guess I was pretty mad because I tossed him out in the street with one hand. As I was doing that Donna reacted very quickly. She began yelling, "Robber, robber, robber," and if that wasn't bad enough, she began hitting one of the men with a basket she was carrying. The street was very crowded, and the bystanders started cheering for Donna as she was wailing on the guy with her chicken basket. The craziest part of the whole thing was that two policemen were standing not fifty feet from us as the whole thing took place. We joked for weeks that Donna swung a mean chicken basket.

With the holiday season came the rains. It was different being in the capital and not in the bush when the rains came. Boy, how I remembered the endless days of running the generators and going without clean water. I wasn't really going to miss that. Also, this holiday season brought the Persian Gulf War. It came as a total surprise to us. One day all was well; the next day we were in a meeting at the embassy about security precautions. For our safety, we were told to change our routines and never drive the same route two days in a row. The marines attached to the embassy were guarding the school that Hilary attended, which she thought was pretty cool. There was a very small Muslim population in Zambia, so the officials thought that any threat was minimal. A few days after the embassy meeting a lot of rumors spread that Saddam Hussein's wife and children were staying at a game preserve north of the capital. The Zambian media always gave a distorted view of the war, with the

United States usually portrayed as the villain. I always found it ironic; people in other countries hated our government yet loved our freedom and our currency. In a very short amount of time the war ceased being news, and life went back to normal.

Around the middle of February, Donna began feeling very fatigued. After a week her color began to change. She was becoming quite jaundiced. Her color was a sickly yellow, almost an orange. Our doctor was unable to make a firm diagnosis, except the obvious, that the illness was either a liver problem or was in some way affecting her liver function. He wanted her to be flown right away to South Africa. We talked it over and thought it would be best for her to go to the States.

Two days later I was putting her on a plane to Chicago via London. As we gathered at the airport, her color was worse, and she could hardly walk. In just two days she had deteriorated very rapidly. She found it so hard to say good-bye. In tears she hugged Marily and Hilary. She held on to Ana for some time. I assured her that we would be fine and that she needed to get well as quickly as possible so she could come back to us.

After arriving in Chicago, she was able to call on the phone. She said the airlines took wonderful care of her. They allowed her to board and depart the two different flights early. In London they gave her a hospitality room to rest in until the next flight. She said within a couple of hours she was on the flight home. An appointment had already been made with an infectious disease specialist. His office was just a couple of hours from home, and her brother would help her get back and forth. I felt good that she was home. I had a lot of confidence in the medical care she would get. Almost as important as her medical care, Donna would be with her family.

A few days later she called on the phone. She had been to the doctor. At that point he wasn't quite sure what was going on. He was running a lot of tests and decided that the next step was to conduct a liver biopsy.

He was leaning to either hepatitis-c or a non-specific hepatitis. She told me that she was so weak it was hard for her to walk. She wanted to talk with the girls. When she talked with Ana, it was easy to see that Ana was trying very hard to talk back to her mom. Before Donna could call me again, she was hospitalized for a few days. During this time Marily and Hilary filled in as much as possible. Hilary made extra special effort to keep Ana occupied and happy. Marily was wonderful as she helped make sure that everything in the house kept going. It wasn't like living in the states. In Zambia every piece of clothing, even socks and underclothing, had to be pressed with a steam iron. It wasn't for style or appearance. It was a matter of health. A particularly nasty fly laid its eggs in damp clothing. If you didn't press your clothes with a hot iron, the larva could survive and burrow into your skin. Weeks later you would have itches that finally ended only when the new flies emerged and flew away.

After about two weeks of Donna being gone, I was involved in some strategic planning meetings. After lunch the first day I began experiencing horrendous back pain. I knew it wasn't muscular or vertebra pain, I had experienced those before. A very short time after the back pain I began to sweat profusely. By the end of the first day I felt lousy and tired. The next morning I was hardly able to crawl out of bed. The back pain began again, and I knew that something was very wrong. I went to the same doctor that tried to treat Donna. He ran a couple of tests and told me that I was probably in the beginning stages of hepatitis-A. He sent me home and told me that I would be in bed for the next four to six weeks if I was lucky. Great! My department didn't need me lying around in bed for a month or more. Well, so much for my sense of self- importance. The next day I had to crawl to my bathroom. I made arrangements for the work in the department to be covered by a couple from the UK. They didn't have much experience in the property area, but they did very well. They allowed the workers to continue their projects, and they made sure that supplies and equipment were available.

Some time after my first week in bed Donna called on the phone. She wanted to talk with me, and I really wanted to talk with her. I got some help getting into the dining room where the phone was. We talked for some time and bantered back and forth about who infected whom. Her doctor told her it would be at least a couple more weeks before she could come back home. She talked with the girls for a while and then told them good-bye. The girls really missed their mom, Ana had no idea what was really going on. What was so hard for me was the fact that I could not spend time with the girls as well. First I was too weak, and then I did not want to spread anything to them. My little Ana went more than a month without her mom, and now I couldn't hold her either.

Slowly the month dragged on, and I was getting a little of my strength back. We were never able to determine the source of the hepatitis. No one else in our family was infected, so we doubted the source was in our home. Donna was due to return to us in a week. It was going to be so good seeing her again. Her girls were really missing her, and I knew she was longing to see them again.

Donna arrived back to us in much better shape than when she left. Even after the biopsy and all of the tests, the doctor was not positive about the cause of her liver troubles. With more than six weeks of complete rest she was able to come home. Everyone was so happy to see her. The men in the building department all came by to greet her and friends from Kankata stopped to greet her as well. But nobody was as happy to see her as the girls and I were. Ana climbed up on her mom's lap and wouldn't move for hours.

Being able to travel around the country was the part of my job that I loved the best. Most of my travels took me to parts of the country where churches were growing. Some of the congregations had outgrown their buildings and needed to expand. Many congregations needed to build for the first time. It was normal for a congregation to meet in the open or in a hut. When they were given land by the village headman, then they could begin to build. The Tonga people in the south of the country were experiencing great growth in their churches. Because of their growth, I was in the south quite a bit. My usual arrangement was to inform the areas that I was coming on a certain day. I would pick up the regional leader, and then we could meet with the people. We would look at each building project and plan its progress and work out the delivery of the supplies that they needed. My office provided the steel door and window frames. The rest was the congregation's responsibility to make or buy.

At one particular location, the men of the church were waiting for us to arrive at their future site. It was an extremely remote area, and most of the people had to walk eight or ten miles to get there. I had picked up their regional leader, Christopher Mabuto, in Mazabuka. Christopher was a marvelous man and a great leader. He led his congregations and his pastors with great vision and care. When we arrived at the site, we were greeted with the usual Tonga respect and friendliness. At the site the people were ready to begin building. They had the property located and even had some very old prints. They had not begun their project because their prints were calculated in feet and inches, not in meters and millimeters. No one around knew how to re-calculate the prints for them. They marveled that it only took a short time to change the plans for them. As soon as I had it done they wanted me to set out the corners and the lines so they could begin digging. I was amazed at their dedication and willingness to work. I thought about how many problems most congregations in the states put themselves through simply because they could not agree or cooperate.

As we left that site and headed on our way, Christopher told me that the people had already baked almost eight thousand bricks. They had been making the bricks out of river clay for over a year. It was usually the women of the congregations that made the bricks. Day after day they would gather at the river bank or creek bed and dig the clay. The clay was then pressed into a crude mold until it firmed up, and then it was set in the sun. When enough bricks had been made, usually five thousand or more, they were baked in a fire. That was done by building igloo type domes out of the bricks. The center of the dome would be hollow. The rows of brick that were being stacked on top of each other were staggered so air and heat could pass between them. When the dome was ready, a fire would be started in the hollow section. The fire would burn for a week or longer, depending on the number of bricks.

Christopher and I continued to the southernmost parts of the country. We were going to visit two more congregations. One congregation was already making progress on their building; the other was just in the planning stages. By the end of the first day, we arrived at the Zimbabwe border where the Zambezi River separates the two countries. Here, Victoria Falls presents a raw and untamed beauty that is unsurpassed in nature.

That night Christopher and I were staying in the pastor's house. It was nice by local standards with two separate bedrooms, kitchen, and living room. By western standards it would be considered sparse and very small. The pastor was very happy to have a house with real floors and a tin roof. Christopher and I would be staying in the small bedroom just off the living room. That night we visited for a while with the pastor and his wife, and then, exhausted, we went to bed. My friend had brought his sleeping bag. I, on the other hand, had forgotten mine. When I was away, I would usually sleep in a jogging suit. I would keep warm, and it kept most of the crawling guests off me. When I used my sleeping bag, I tucked my head down into the bag to keep unwanted visitors off. I imagine because I was so tired, I was asleep as soon as I pulled the covers over my head.

In the middle of the night the sound of something woke me up. At first, I couldn't tell what the noise was or where it was coming from. The glow of the hands on my watch told me it was almost three. As my eyes adjusted to the dark and I tried to focus, the noise came again. It was coming from the wall at the head of our beds. My small bunk was about three feet from Christopher's. Our heads were both near the entrance to the room. Leaning against the wall near the doorway was a steel door frame. I supposed it was going to be used for the building project and this was a safe place to keep it. The noise came again, and I knew that it must be coming from the top of the door frame. I had to turn over to get a good look, and when I did, I was looking at a rat about as big as a two- or three-month-old kitten. As a kid I had seen some pretty big sewer rats, and this one could be a cousin. He was sitting on top of the frame, looking down on Christopher and me. Well, me he could recognize, but Christopher was inside his sleeping bag.

As I watched the critter, he demonstrated to me his noise-making capability. He was gnawing his front teeth on the metal door frame. I didn't know if he was sharpening them for dinner or what. I didn't want to find out. I whispered Christopher's name a few times to try and rouse him. I figured if I had to stare at that chisel-toothed rodent, then my friend was going to as well. Christopher finally stirred and looked my way. When he did, I pointed up to the metal chewing intruder. And when he saw the rat, he didn't hesitate a millisecond to put his head back under his sleeping bag. Lucky for him, in a second the rat jumped from his spot onto my unsuspecting and hiding friend, and a split-second later he jumped from my now petrified comrade to the window about five feet away. As I stared at the rat, Christopher tried to dig his way through the bed and get under it. And from there, our visitor, my Welcome-to-Vic-Falls Emissary, simply darted out a hole in the glass. Needless to say, I did not sleep or even close my eyes the rest of the night. My good friend, on the other hand, was back asleep in a few minutes. It was easy to tell who the rookie was that night.

That morning it was easy to see the reason for our nighttime visitor. Behind the houses all of the garbage was piled into big mounds. There was no sanitation department in the cities and villages so all of the refuse got dumped outside. Some people buried their refuse, and some didn't. The rats had the run of the place as soon as the sun went down. At Kankata we had burned what we could, and the rest was buried. The same was true living in Lusaka: we burned and buried. But not here.

Our last stop before heading home was a church located in a town area owned by a coal mining company. The congregation had begun building months before our arrival. The leader of the building committee was the head of the company's fire department. He was a friendly man who had dedicated hundreds of hours to the building. We were to meet him and schedule the delivery of the door and window frames. Scheduling a truck to travel that far was the biggest problem. To make it feasible, the truck would have to make deliveries along the way.

With the cost of fuel going up weekly our budget could be exhausted in no time. So each trip had to be planned very carefully and the truck loaded to the maximum. There were times when we would have to wait months for supplies to arrive for our projects. Of all of the supplies that were the most critical and the most difficult to get, it had to be bags of cement. At one point we went almost six months without cement. When we could buy it, we bought it by the hundreds of bags. Then it would be stored in containers, the type that came off ocean-going ships. The containers could be locked and were pretty weather resistant. I learned a lesson in improvising the first time I took cement to a site. The empty cement bags are valuable, even sell-able. The cement bags were used by the local people as toilet paper. In the bush there was no such thing as Charmin. So whenever we shipped cement out to the bush, there were always people willing to unload; they got first dibs on the TP.

a mother's courage

∧∧∧

ith another rainy season coming to an end, we were anxious to get back to Ana's village. We had been able to talk about adoption, and we felt that the family understood what we wanted to do. On our last visit before the rains Dominic told us that he still wanted Ana to come back. Donna and I continued to pray that he would understand why Ana was doing so well in her current environment with our family. I thought if he understood, he would want her to stay with us.

Donna had been back home now about two months. Her bout with hepatitis had left her very weak, but she felt strong enough now to make the trip out to the village. On this trip we wanted to have a serious discussion about Ana.

We left Lusaka early in the morning and headed straight to Mazabuka. We were going to pick up Mr. Chibamba, who worked for the Child Welfare Office. We met him earlier, and he agreed to travel with us to the village. He was going to try and help the family, especially Dominic, understand what adoption was all about.

As we traveled the two hours to the village, he told us that adoption was almost unheard of in the remote areas of the country. We would be breaking new ground as we tried to adopt Ana. We arrived at the village with the usual greetings from the children, who were always happy to see us. On this trip we brought a bag of oranges. We bought them at the duty-free shop in Lusaka. Oranges were not grown in Zambia, so they had to be shipped up from the south. Well, the children just loved the oranges. Hilary showed them how to put an orange wedge in their mouth and smile. When they did it, they just laughed and laughed at each other.

The older women remarked again at how well Ana was doing. She was walking and getting around pretty well, considering that the rickets had bowed her legs like pretzels. When she walked, she tottered from side to side. After a while all of the adults sat down to talk. We had already introduced Mr. Chibamba, who had been talking to some of the women since our arrival. He interpreted everything for us as the conversations happened. He told Dominic that it was easy to see love. He told him to look at our family, see how they loved each other, and see how our family love had already included Ana. She was a part of this family. And then he told Dominic and the others that making Ana live in the village would kill her, and that making her come back would be taking her from her Momma and Papa.

Our conversation lasted for some time. At one point, the consent form was talked about. Both Donna and I felt we were very close to having permission for the adoption. We had been talking for almost an hour. Dominic was talking quietly with the older women. Donna was holding Ana, and I was talking with Mr. Chibamba. After a few minutes we came back together. Dominic told us it was easy to see our love for Ana. Then he talked about all of the wonderful blessings she would enjoy if we adopted her. She would have good food and clothes. When she was sick, she would have good medicines, and she would be able to learn many things. After saying all of that, he uttered the words our hearts had been straining to hear: "I will let you adopt her." We were so happy we almost cried right there. Mr. Chibamba explained that the consent form would have to be signed in the presence of the magistrate in Mazabuka. It was going to take one more trip, and the adoption process could begin.

Donna and I left the village on clouds. Our little angel was going to be a permanent part of our family. Our hearts and souls would never have to worry about her living in the village. She would be our Ana Syoma Galloway. "Thank you, Lord, for all of the prayers that you answered." We dropped off our new friend, Mr. Chibamba, at his home and thanked him over and over for his help. When he got out of the truck, he handed me the blue consent form.

As soon as we got back home, we set a date to go back. It would be a couple of weeks. We sent word to Dominic when we would return to the village. The people had a very reliable method of passing along messages. It was simply by word-of-mouth. People traveling and talking would pass messages along as efficiently as Western Union. We also sent word to our friend Moffat, at Kankata, who would be traveling with us.

The two weeks went by so slowly. Negative thoughts tried to creep into our minds. What if he changes his mind? What if he wants Ana back right away? We reminded ourselves of the answers to prayer that we were standing on. How many times did my heart take me back to that rainy night? How many times did I replay Donna's tears and her words thanking Jesus that Ana was still breathing?

The day came for us to pick up Moffat and head to the village. He was waiting for us with his infectious smile and polite Tonga greeting. Moffat wanted us to go by a slightly different route this particular morning. It was a beautiful morning, and our spirits were soaring. The journey couldn't be fast enough for me.

As we traveled, I had to negotiate a rather dangerous gully. It was about four feet deep and about as wide. I got out and looked and felt pretty sure that the truck would span the gully if I went very slowly. Well, I thought I did everything right, but things went very wrong. In an instant the truck was on its side. The passenger side of the truck was on the bottom of the gully. My full-size double-cab truck was at about a sixty-degree angle on its side.

Moffat opened his door and climbed out. I handed Ana out the window to him. Donna had to climb over the seat and climb out the open door. A fine mess we were in, hours from any help, and it had to happen today. Moffat thought that I might be able to drive the truck out of the gully. He would have to engage the front hubs to lock in the four-wheel drive. That was easy for him to do on my side of the truck. On the passenger side, though, the hub was partially buried in the dirt. With his chest pressed against the front tire, he had to reach around and lock in the hub. After digging a little he had the hub locked in, and he climbed out. I was thinking that this would make one fantastic commercial if it worked. Slowly, very slowly, I inched the truck forward, hoping that the tires would be able to grip enough. And, lo and behold, it did. In a few moments, the truck was out and sitting on flat ground. We were on our way again.

The children heard the truck coming long before we got there. As we crested the hill in front of the village, they were waiting for us. I remember some of the times when children in some of the remote areas ran away from me screaming. The rural Tonga people still taught their children that everybody was born black. The more you sinned, the more evil you were, and the lighter your skin became. So in the eyes of some of the children I was an evil giant.

After the greetings we headed on to Mazabuka and the magistrate. The trip would take a couple of hours. Moffat and Ana's father talked quietly in the language of Tonga for a little while. Donna and I were left alone with our own quiet thoughts. I was simply imagining what I assumed was going to happen. Dominic would sign the consent form in front of the magistrate, and this chapter in Ana's life would draw to a close as another would begin. I could only imagine what was going through Donna's mind, each thought activating a response in her heart and soul. She had been through so much with Ana: the seizures that almost ended her struggle and now her badly bowed legs. The news from the doctors always seemed dismal, void of much hope that Ana would enjoy a normal life. Deep down, I knew it was the Lord that enabled Donna to care the way she did.

A couple of hours later we arrived in Mazabuka. It is a fairly large town with a police station and a few shops. We found some cold Cokes and then went to the magistrate's office. Her office was very sparse, three old chairs and her desk. The windows on one side of the room had no glass, and the curtains were old and bleached by the sun. She greeted us and invited us in. Donna and Dominic sat in the two chairs, so I stood beside Donna and Ana, with Moffat standing a little behind me. I was getting a little anxious as the magistrate talked about trivial things. Finally, she got down to business. She asked Dominic some questions about Ana and her birth mother. Then, she asked Donna how long we had been taking care of Ana. Donna told her that it had been almost two years.

At this point she picked up the blue consent form and asked Dominic if he understood the form and did he fully understand what it meant for us to adopt Ana. In a very low voice, he told her that he had never heard of adoption and had no intention of giving up his daughter. He finished by telling her that when Ana was healthy, he wanted to take her back.

I couldn't believe what he just said. His words left my mind staggering. This man whom we had talked with about Ana was now cutting out my heart. He knew that if she were to go back, it would just be a matter of time before he would have to bury her. He knew there was no food and the other children were sick. My chest started hurting and I was having trouble getting my breath. The room was closing in on me, and I had to get some air. I headed towards the door when I heard Donna's voice. I was on the verge of tears. Moffat, too, was visibly shaken.

Donna stood up from her chair holding onto Ana. Ana was dressed in just her diaper and a simple pullover dress. The room was silent, and the tension was as stifling as the heat. The heat just added to my breathing difficulties. Donna took off Ana's dress and laid it on the chair. She then unpinned her diaper and laid it on the chair as well. I thought, "What is she doing? What is happening?" In a second, she uttered the most heart-wrenching words I can ever remember hearing. With Ana undressed she handed her over to Dominic and said, "If you want her back, you must take her from me now. I give her back to you the way that she came to me." I wasn't just hearing the words come from Donna's mouth; I was experiencing the weight and consequence of every one of them.

This was the most incredible act of courage a mother's heart could perform. At this point tears were streaming down my face. Moffat was in tears as well. The woman who nursed this child on the verge of death, who sat up nights holding her as she convulsed and struggled just to stay alive, was giving her back to her birth father. I wanted to shout, "Wait a minute, I've been a father to her. I took her swimming for the first time. She is a part of my heart. Don't give her back!"

As if repulsed by some force Dominic jumped back away from Donna's extended arms. "I can't take her back right now," he said. Donna told him again that he would have to take Ana right now. And, again he refused. At this point the magistrate interrupted the scene. She told us that we would need to take this matter to the Supreme Court. And since we had taken care of her for so long, the court would grant us the adoption. At her words Dominic moved away from us and towards the windows. I was able to gain my composure, and Donna put Ana's clothes back on her. Without many more words we left the office.

The ride back to the village was horrendous. Dominic never uttered a word the entire trip. The small talk between Donna and me was just to mask our pain and the devastation in our souls. Could all of the tears and sleepless nights be for nothing? How can this man play with such a young life, as if she were some pawn on a chess board? He knows we love her as our own flesh. During the ride back Moffat was very quiet. He spoke once to Dominic and once or twice to us. He took this very hard.

We approached the village, and the children were waiting. I stopped the truck, wondering what I should say to Dominic. He got out of the truck before I could speak. Usually we would have stopped long enough to be respectful and then say goodbye. I didn't plan on being there that long. This time I wanted to leave with Ana and never come back. I didn't want Ana ever to see the village again. As I began to back out, Moffat told me to stop. I stopped the truck and turned it off. Moffat was listening to the conversations going on behind one of the huts. The elderly women were talking with Dominic. Moffat told us the conversation was getting pretty hot. The women were accusing him of wanting to sell the baby to the Americans. He was denying that, and they returned with, "Then why won't you sign the paper? Do you want her blind like her brother, or with no hair?" It was very quiet; even the children were still. In a moment Dominic was walking towards us with his head a little bowed towards the ground. He came up on the passenger side of the truck and told us that he would sign the paper as soon as we could go back to Mazabuka.

Talk about being confused! In Mazabuka my heart was torn out. I drove back to the village not even able to talk with Donna. And now this: "I will sign the papers." I knew in a few hours it would be dark, and we had to head back. Nobody wanted to drive the roads once the sun went down. They were very dangerous at night. Car thieves armed with automatic weapons rode around looking for victims. Abandoned trucks with no lights or reflectors could be around any curve. I knew that because we lost a friend who was killed when he rammed into the back end of a semi-trailer with no lights or warning signals.

We left the village in a mixed state of confusion, resolve, and a sense of God's involvement in the entire situation. We were confused at Dominic's behavior. We were resolved to do whatever it would take to adopt Ana. We knew that the Lord was in the middle of these events, even when we could only cry and suffer broken hearts. The drive back was quiet, and we arrived just before dusk. We dropped off our dear friend and headed for home. The dusk was like flames dancing on the horizon. The landscape was beautiful with its huge Baobab trees, their trunks bigger than cars. The wonderfully intoxicating landscape began its work on my weary soul.

grandma and hotdogs

∧∧∧

e had been living in Zambia for almost two years. It was time for us to go home for our vacation. We would have eight wonderful weeks with our family and friends. Grandma had stayed healthy, and she was eager to see us. Donna had been telling her and all of the family about our little Ana and how much of a blessing she was. Donna's oldest brother made arrangements for us to have a house for the summer. It was out in the country, which would be nice. Also, it was pretty close to town, which would make it easy for shopping and going to church.

Our flight was to take us to London, with a short stop in New York before going on to Chicago. Making the arrangements for Ana's travel papers went without any problems. Even up to this point, with all of the traveling we did going into Zimbabwe, we were never once questioned about custody matters. Now with her visitor's visa on her papers, we were ready to go.

Marily and Hilary began telling Ana about her Grandma—how she made the best chocolate chip cookies and strawberry jam. Our little girl had come such a long way. The wonderful miracle that began that rainy night was continuing to unfold for everybody to see. Even though Ana's legs were still terribly bowed because of the rickets, she was walking well. She was looking forward to seeing her Grandma. She was talking pretty well. I was her "Papa," and Donna was her "Mummy." She could also pronounce her sisters' names pretty well. The girls wondered how Ana would react to her Grandma for the first time.

We arrived at the airport in plenty of time prior to departure. Our flight was bound for London. We would have a few hours to spend in Heathrow Airport. We boarded the plane and thought that each of us would have a seat, including Ana. We were wrong; Ana would have to be on Donna's lap with a special seat belt. When we were airborne, then Ana could be unbuckled but have to stay on one of our laps. When it was time to sleep, they gave Donna a soft- sided sleeping box that would lie across the top of her seat. It would lie on the armrest and extend a couple of inches over the next seat. Ana could hardly fit in it.

The flight to London was exciting. We knew that in a matter of a few hours we would be with family and friends. However, the flight was pretty stressful on Donna and Ana. Ana was so excited about seeing Grandma that she was a bundle of energy. She didn't want to sleep, and everybody else on the entire plane did. At the end of the flight, a young mother traveling with two perfect angels— they seemed to sleep the entire trip—told Donna her secret for long distance travel: "Give your child a dose of Visteril about an hour before the flight." She told Donna it worked every time.

We stayed in Heathrow and wandered around for a while. It had only been two years, and so many things were different. It was a shock to see the shelves packed with so many items. We had forgotten how blessed the western world really was. In a little while we boarded our flight for New York. It seemed like a quick flight, and we gained a few hours on the clock. In New York we didn't have much time and went right away to our Chicago connection. Once airborne on our way to Chicago, we were really excited. In just a couple of hours we would be in very familiar territory and on our way to the great north.

We landed in Chicago and made arrangements with our regional office to use a car for the summer. After taking care of a few other required business items, we wanted to be on our way. How was Grandma going to react? All of us had changed so much. Marily was taller and slender. Hilary was a few inches taller, and her golden hair was even longer. Both Donna and I had lost weight. Grandma had only been able to see a couple of pictures of all of us, and that was when Donna was home with her liver problems.

After loading up the car, we were off to the great north of Michigan. We were no longer exhausted, pumped up on the excitement of being home. It would be impossible to count how many times I had driven these roads on our way home. Wherever we had lived, northern Michigan was home. We had been so blessed to be able to spend almost every Christmas with Grandma, that is, before moving to Zambia. Vacation time was always spent in the north. Swimming in Lake Huron and late-night campfires were sweet memories hidden in our hearts. Every vacation we would take Grandma for rides, and on each trip we would stop and buy cheese, crackers, and a northern Michigan favorite, pickled bologna. Lunch time was always pulled over on a dirt road enjoying our wonderful lunch, usually graced by passing deer and chattering squirrels.

The ride home seemed to take forever. Familiar landmarks told us we were getting ever closer, yet it seemed to be taking longer than any of us remembered. The last couple of hours consisted of roadways lined with majestic pines and beautiful farmland, the pines reaching into the sky and the farm land dotted with bales of hay or new planted corn. One of the most famous trout streams in the world, the beautiful Au

Sable River, was just miles from home. Just south of home we crossed over the river and knew we were very close. It would be about another hour. Donna and the girls started singing all of the silly camp songs they knew. Countless times as we got close to Grandma's, they would sing the camp songs like "Cannibal King," "Shuffling Horatio," "My Tall Silk Hat," "I'm a Little Pile of Tin," and many others. They were going to teach their little sister to sing them as well. For the next hour they taught Ana songs that had brought so much childhood joy to their own hearts.

The last couple of miles it was non-stop talk about Grandma. We pulled into the parking lot of her apartment complex, and the girls were out of the car like they were shot out of a cannon. They opened Grandma's door, and Marily and Hilary were giving hugs and kisses. Ana came into the apartment and without missing a step crawled up onto Grandma's lap. "Hi Grandma," she said. It was like they had seen each other only yesterday. Grandma seemed a little surprised. We sat and talked for a couple of hours and then headed to our home for the summer.

It only took about fifteen minutes to get to the house. It was very nice, and we felt very blessed to have someone allow us to live in their home. The owners were wonderful Christians that had been involved in some short-term mission work in their congregation. They were going to spend the summer at their cabin and on their boat. The house was cozy, and we settled right in. It was so nice to be home, to be with our family.

A few days after coming home, we celebrated Donna's birthday. We were going to have a big cookout and had invited all of our family. At the party I cooked hot dogs and hamburgers on the grill. They smelled wonderful. At the party Ana would meet her very best friend. Our nephew and his family came to the party. Ashley, his youngest, came and met Ana. They became instant friends and stuck to each other the entire time. At the party Ana ate her first hot dog. They quickly became her favorite summer food.

It was so nice being back in Northern Michigan. During the week we would spend time with family and friends. On weekends we would visit some of the churches that we had served. It was always a blessing to visit with friends that shared our faith. In every town we lived, there were special people that loved us and that we loved in return. Our friends remarked at how much Hilary had grown and how Marily was such a lovely young woman. I was so proud of my girls. They were such a blessing to me and Donna. And, Ana, well, she charmed everyone she met with her smile and loving spirit. Her personality was infectious.

But not all was rosy. One incident was particularly disturbing that summer. Donna was approached by a minister who attended school with us. She was African American and had a very negative view about us having Ana. She almost accused us of wanting to adopt Ana because we looked at ourselves as some type of savior to the Africans. That type of thinking really hurt us. She seemed to be saying it was okay to talk about loving each other as Jesus loved us, but we must keep it within some reasonable or socially acceptable boundary. We knew that Ana was a gift to us and that God restored her life for a specific purpose. We were just the people who had been tremendously privileged to care for her. I wondered when we would ever be able to live in a color-blind world.

The summer moved all too quickly for us. Soon we were scheduled for our physical check-ups and the preparation to head back to Zambia. A few days after visiting the clinic, Donna was called by our doctor. Her chest x-ray revealed some spots on her lung. The doctor wasn't sure what they were, and he wanted her checked out. It was very close to the time for us to leave, and now something was wrong with Donna's lungs. She was scheduled to see a specialist to determine what the spots were and their cause. Our departure would have to be delayed until the test results were in and she was cleared to go back.

Donna began a four-week period of testing and waiting. Trying to determine the cause of the spots on her lung was going to be difficult.

Donna and the kids spent most of this time with her mom, and I was going out to a friend's house out in the country. He had a small apple orchard of about 1,200 trees. It was the end of August, and the apples were becoming ripe and ready to pick. Quite a few days of the week I would go out to the orchard and pick apples for him. With fall coming the mornings were cool and the dew heavy. There is no better time to be in the north. The most gifted artist in the world could not do justice to the living canvas that I enjoyed. The maple trees were a flame with their reds and oranges. The Ida Reds that hung from the trees were brilliant tones of red, and the Empires were almost a deep crimson. I loved every moment that I had in that orchard. I picked hundreds of bushels of apples and relished every second in that created world of reds and oranges, a world filled with the smell of the morning dew and ripe apples.

While I was taking trips out to the orchard, the doctors were able to determine the cause of the spots on Donna's lung. Well, they thought they were pretty sure. They thought they were caused by a parasite that probably invaded her lung the same time her liver problem developed. After a lot of questioning, they built a time- line and came to a reasonable conclusion:

On one of her visits to a rural area she had eaten some bad goat meat. Her friend from Canada went with her, and it was their custom to have lunch if it was offered. A little while later we learned that our Canadian friend had a very serious bowel problem that was caused by parasites and had to have a section of her bowel removed. I guess that it was one of the risks that we took when we went out into the bush. There were times when we visited in the villages that we would eat with the people. It really depended on the condition of the village. If things were very bleak for the people, we never ate, because what we ate would take away from somebody else. Most of the time it was the children or their mothers who went without.

Well, with the news from the doctors, we were cleared to go back. We were excited about returning to our work and the wonderful people that we worked with. I loved working in the Property Department. The men working with me were wonderful and caring. I appreciated their dedication to their work and tried to show them. We made sure that while we were on vacation we got each of them something special. They were convinced that America was the best land in the world.

About a week before returning, a strange thing happened to me. I was feeling deep inside that something was very wrong and that we should not return. I couldn't put my finger on it. I was never a superstitious person and didn't give much credence to premonitions. Yet, I could not shake free from this inner voice telling me that something very wrong was going to happen. I didn't tell anybody about what I was feeling. I didn't want to alarm Donna with feelings that had no rational justification. I was praying that as God called us to Zambia He was going to take care of us every step of the way.

Our wonderful family saw us off again, and we were on our way back to the land of the Baobab and Jacaranda trees. After the usual two-day flight we landed back in Zambia. Everyone in our department was glad to see us. They all told me that I got fat and the girls were more beautiful than before we left. After a couple of days of adjustment we were back in the swing of things and the flow of Zambian life.

the unthinkable happens

∧∧∧

"He beat me." Donna's words were just above a whisper. She was standing in front of me, both of her wrists were a deep red and beginning to swell. Her blouse and jumper were ripped in a long jagged tear. Turning around she moved her blouse, displaying a deep red, almost purple, fist sized imprint in the center of her back. Donna, my wife, partner in ministry, the mother of our children, caregiver to the sick, stood in front of me shaking. Her look was dazed; she seemed almost in a stupor. Her usual energy filled voice was no more than a faint whisper. I needed to find out what was going on. I had spent some time in my office and had been in the house for just a few minutes. It was New Year's Eve, and we were planning on having a cookout with some friends. It still seemed strange cooking outside in December. Donna was out looking after the reported need of a little child, I couldn't count how many times a knock on our door summoned Donna to help a sick child or a hurt or wounded adult.

Slowly, in a quiet hushed voice, like she was going to reveal some great secret, she told me that it was Pastor Chibolio, from the education center, who attacked and beat her. And in fact, it was in front of his wife and onlookers, that he very calmly locked the front door and attacked and beat her. She told me, "In a cold, monotone voice, he told me that I was a woman who needed to be beaten and he was going to beat me." Donna's voice and face were expressionless. The words came out of her mouth like some recorded message.

Again, she said, "He told me that I needed to be beaten and that he was going to do it. He was so close to me I could feel his breath as he talked. And then he walked over and closed and bolted the door. I told him he was making a mistake. While I was talking to him I tried to back towards the door and thought I might be able to unbolt the slide on the lock. And then his wife came over and tried to stop him, and he threw her against the wall." Now with tears running down her cheeks and beginning to shake she said, "Tedd, people were watching through the windows of the house as he pressed me against the door." She told me the names of some who were watching through the windows. They were some of the very people that she helped when their children were sick. Again she said, "They watched everything, they saw him press his body against me and tell me he was going to beat me and they didn't try to help me. A man who doesn't even live on our compound was sitting on the couch reading a newspaper and watching Chibolio beat me, like he was watching something on TV."

Even after a couple of minutes of telling me about being attacked Donna was still talking in a whisper. I tried to understand more of what happened and asked her what else she remembered. She said, "While he was pressing his body against me, Mrs. Chenda must have come in the back door. She came up behind Chibolio and grabbed me by the arm and pulled me away from him. As I was getting away from him he punched me so hard in the back that it knocked me to the floor."

And now, just minutes later she is standing in front of me with ripped blouse, wrists already beginning to swell and a fist-sized red imprint on her back.

I was confused and in shock. Why did this happen? What did Donna ever do to anyone to deserve this? I tried to get her to talk a little more about what took place. Pastor Chibolio told her our dog, Nimrod, bit his daughter on the foot and she must come over right away and treat her. Again, that was not unusual, for Donna was the one whom people called all of the time. At this point in our stay she had already delivered two babies, both in my truck, and had visited the squalor-filled workers' compounds numerous times. Just visiting the compounds was a great risk. In the rainy season the pit-latrines ran over into the streets, and hundreds of people died of cholera. So, as the wonderful, caring person that she is, off she went to the pastor's house.

On the bottom of the little girl's foot was a small scratch almost healed and about one inch long. It was obvious that our dog never bit her. The pastor was insisting that Donna take his daughter to the University Hospital and be treated. Donna tried to explain to him that the hospital would not even have a topical antibiotic to give her. Almost instantly I knew he used this trumped up incident to lure Donna to his house. It was at this time that he confronted her and closed and bolted the door.

I knew I needed to get Donna to a doctor as fast as I could. I didn't know if she had any other injuries. I took her over to another administrator's house and informed her of what happened and that I was taking Donna to the doctor. We walked the hundred yards back to our house, so I could tell the girls what I was doing.

As we approached the gate to our yard, Chibolio came up about twenty yards behind us. He yelled at us and then started taunting Donna. Over and over again he was hollering, "You want me, woman, don't you? You know you want me." As he taunted Donna, he pointed his fingers towards his body and made gestures. Donna tried to lunge out of my arms; she wanted to go after him. I was not about to let her go. I knew I wanted to get my hands on the creep. What kind of a man would act this way? I also knew very clearly that if I reacted to him and a confrontation took place it could get very ugly and dangerous real fast. My entire family could be in grave peril. My home could be burned down, my children injured and Ana taken away. It is sad to say, but mob violence is the rule and not the exception. Well, with all of my might I got Donna into my truck. As her attacker was approaching me, I called him a dirty pig and told him to get out of my way. I guess the tone of my voice conveyed the message that I was not messing around.

In the capital there was only one clinic that served westerners. I pulled into the clinic parking lot and parked the truck. Donna was still dazed and somewhat confused. The doctor was available and took us in right away. He examined Donna and told her that both wrists were severely sprained from the grip of her attacker. He assured us that in a week or so the physical signs of the attack would lessen. He told us that we should go right away and inform the Zambian police and that we should take his report with us. We had decided not to tell him that her attacker was a minister who lived on the same compound we did. We also knew that once we reported this to the police, the consequences would be severe and inhumane. I knew what they routinely did to men accused of crimes. One form of interrogation involved being tied upside down to a grate. Then the bottoms of the suspect's feet were beaten with either a piece of hose or wood. The guilty would confess, and the innocent would beg for mercy. Two of our guards were once accused of theft, and their feet were beaten so badly that one of them had to be carried home and could not work for a month. At this point we didn't know what we wanted to happen to Chibolio.

When we left the clinic I knew that we must inform our denominational leader. As it was a holiday I knew she would be home.

I drove straight to her house and she asked us to come in. She could tell by looking at us that something was wrong. After Donna told her what took place, she was livid. She told us that she would deal with it immediately. We left her feeling that it would be dealt with justly. We both knew that we needed to get away from the compound for a while. I didn't really know what I would do if I saw Chibolio again. We needed to think and pray about what happened and how it would affect our family and ministry. We stopped at our house long enough to get some clothes and the girls. We headed to Zimbabwe, to our friends at the Most High retreat center. For two days we talked and prayed about what happened and how it might affect us.

We also knew that in order for us to stay in Zambia some form of punitive action must be taken with Chibolio. We wrote a letter to our leader and requested some actions be taken. The first, he should be removed from preaching and teaching privileges while he was to receive counseling. We both thought six months would be a beginning point; after all, if he were convicted publicly, he would be in jail for a lot longer than that. The second action was to look into his background and see if he had a history of violence towards women. When we left Most High we felt that we were being more than fair, in fact, lenient.

Upon arriving back in Zambia I gave the letter to our leader. After reading it she seemed very quiet, a moment later she told me she would consider our request. She also told me that the pastor did confess to what he had done, almost too every point that Donna had reported. She concluded by telling us that he told her he beat and attacked Donna because we were prejudiced. Her words, that we were prejudiced, hurt us deeply. We wanted the people around us to understand that God's love placed in a person's heart can make a person color-blind. Could people really think we were prejudiced? We loved the people around us, and in our hearts we knew we were not prejudiced.

Coming back into Zambia we decided to speak to a good friend who was the doctor at the American Embassy. He spoke to Donna and me and expressed great concern for Donna's mental health. An attack on a woman by a person who was supposed to be trusted leaves tremendous pain and scars. After talking he did something very unexpected, he offered us his home for a week or so as he and his wife would be out of the country. His gesture to us was overwhelming and with heart-felt thanks we accepted the offer. We left the embassy and went home to gather a few things.

I continued to go to the office the week we stayed in our friend's home. Donna stayed behind with the girls and rested. In just a couple of days it became clear that the administration was not going to do anything about the attack on Donna. There were not going to be any restrictions on his teaching, nor was he going to be required to have counseling. It was at this time that I learned that Pastor Chibolio had been kept out of Bible College for past abusive actions. It was hard for me to believe that the church knew of his past actions and still allowed him to attend our seminary and become an ordained minister.

We were stumbling through our days numb, in shock and becoming more detached from an administration that seemed more concerned about appearances to the outside world than about moral truth and redemptive discipline. By any standard what happened to Donna was a crime and grievous sin. To not administer church discipline was a sin as well. Ignoring what happened was not going to make it go away, nor was it going to prevent it from happening to another innocent victim.

I was beginning to sense that Donna was coming close to some type of collapse. One day, I found her sitting on the floor in our office area with her back against a door. She was weeping and seemed unable to move. With her hands over her ears and tears rolling down her cheeks she whispered to me, "Is he still out there? I can't go out there." Apparently he had been speaking to someone in the same tone of voice that he used when he attacked Donna. I didn't know how much more Donna could take without something terrible happening.

I asked to have a meeting with our denominational head. She had been in Zambia for almost a year. She had years of missionary service, mostly in African nations. She was a very respectable British person who kept her emotions in check and self-disclosure to an absolute minimum. I wanted to discuss our future and the difficulties we were having. She told us that when she was in Biafra she had to deal with a lot of unpleasant situations. And, at one time there were riots and gunfire, and that she just kept a stiff upper lip and went on. I must say that she was the epitome of British stoicism. Her wire-rimmed glasses, combined with her cold, matter-of-fact British tone, left both of us feeling rather dazed. The meeting was a disaster and ended when she told Donna that if she would just apologize to Chibolio the matter would go away. I knew in my heart that I was going to have to seek a meeting with a much higher authority.

Later that week, I requested a meeting with the person in charge of the denomination's work on the African continent. The minister was coming to Zambia the first weekend in February, from our International Office in London. I requested a meeting with him, and was told that if there was time, we could meet. I knew that some type of change needed to take place.

A week before our meeting, I found a letter in my mail box. The letter was from Chibolio, Donna's attacker. It was addressed to the denominational leader with a copy to me. In the letter he informed her that he was reporting us to the government and would have us deported immediately. And that since she had not dealt with our prejudice, he would take matters into his own hands. The letter was filled with all kinds of hateful language about kicking all of the white people out of his country, beginning with the Americans. After reading the letter I went to the administrator's office to discuss it. She was holding the original in her hand as we spoke. The conversation only added to my frustration. I decided I would not talk to Donna about the letter until later.

Donna's ability to cope with even the most basic responsibilities was evaporating in the heat of stress. She couldn't focus on her work. She was retreating from things in her life that she enjoyed. To make matters worse, threats had been made against Marily and Hilary. The rumors came around that if the girls were found outside the safety of the compound they would get the same treatment that their mother got. Our guards who worked the front security gate pledged to take care of the girls and keep them safe. They loved Donna and the girls because Donna took such good care of their children when they were ill.

As if all of this wasn't enough, Donna was told by the woman pastor responsible for women's ministries that she had better be careful. She came to Zambia with two children, and she may only have two when she leaves. Her veiled threats revealed the prejudice in her heart. She had come from Zimbabwe and many people were actually frightened of her. More and more I knew that Donna might collapse any day from the stress.

The weekend with our London leader had arrived, and we were going to have our meeting. He seemed like a very kind and compassionate man. He had served in Africa for many years. And, he understood the stress that missionaries had to deal with. We met in our administrator's office. After a few minutes of small talk it was time to talk about "the incident," the label our leader had put on it. The gentleman from London suggested we consider an appointment in South Africa. I told him we would be glad to discuss that. Well, we never had the chance. What happened in the next few moments changed things forever. Our leader, in her proper British tone and stiff upper lip, told Donna again that if she would just apologize, the whole situation would go away. Those cold and insensitive words cut so deep into my wife's mind and spirit that she began a terrifying period that could only be described as a breakdown.

In an instant Donna was out of her seat and heading out of the office. I quickly got up and followed her the hundred yards to our house. As I came into the house, I found her holding on to a baseball bat and saying, "Yeah. I'll go and apologize." I put my arms around her, and she collapsed onto the floor. Curled like a child, she began to quietly weep. I sat her up on the floor, and she began to rock back and forth very slowly. After a few minutes I managed to get her up and onto the couch. As I sat on the couch with my dear wife, it was evident that she was detached from everything around her. Her stare was blank, and a very quiet and disturbing sound was coming from inside her. She wasn't crying or moaning; it was a very sad and heart rending whimper, coming from deep within her. With the blank expression and the soul-troubling sound coming from my wife, I thought that I had lost her forever.

As I sat there with Donna, the gentleman from London came into the house. He sat down on the chair across from us. As he sat, his wife came in and sat next to Donna. She put her arms around Donna and just held her for a moment. It was obvious to them, by the look on their faces, that they were very concerned about Donna. Things were very quiet for a few minutes as Donna just sat and continued to rock very slowly and tear me apart by the cry from her soul. I asked to speak with our guest from London and we went into the dining room to talk. At this point, my composure was coming apart and with anger welling up inside I told him that he must make immediate arrangements for Donna, Hilary, and Ana to be on the next available flight to the states.

Within the hour, the arrangements were being made. The meeting that just took place happened on a Friday, and by Monday afternoon all of the plans were in place. The American Embassy issued a visa for Ana right away. Our friend, the embassy doctor, cut through all of the red-tape and we had Ana's Visitor Visa within hours. I wanted to make sure that Donna knew her girls were going to be safe and on their way with her.

On Tuesday, we loaded up a few things for the flight back to the states. As we prepared to leave a few of our Zambian friends gathered around us. Some of my men were in tears, the men who pledged to protect our girls were weeping openly and in distress. Anna, our beautiful friend who gave her heart and time to Ana, Marily, and Hilary was crying and holding on to Ana. Ana seemed upset and yet a little puzzled as to what was going on. In the midst of all of the tears I knew we had to go. Last minute hugs and prayer for a safe journey and to the airport we headed. Donna was still not doing well, she seemed weak and still a little unsure of all that was happening. I knew that she was still in a state of shock. Our friend at the embassy told me that she could suffer from the trauma and shock for weeks or longer.

Our farewell was tearful and excruciating. I was going to worry for the next two days about their flights and arrival home. My heart was filled with sorrow, though at the same time a bit of relief. Donna was now safe, Ana was beyond the reach of evil people, and little Hilary wouldn't be threatened anymore. I prayed that they would be taken care of when they arrived in Chicago.

trying to cope

arily and I returned from the airport. I was empty and confused. Questions filled my mind, ready to consume me. What was happening to us? All we wanted for the past ten years of our life was to fulfill our calling to the mission field. I felt like I was almost blind and trying to find my way down a very dark path at midnight, with the path zigzagging in every direction as it went up and down steep hills. I thought I was coming near a breaking point myself. I guess that most people that know me would say that I was a peaceful and calming influence. And, that I was a person of strength and stability. I knew that I had to hold things together. Marily was depending on me here in Zambia, and Donna and the other girls needed the reassurance that I was all right.

Marily proved what a marvelous young lady she is. She never complained about things. Most of her friends had money and a car; she had neither. Even when we were in the bush, she took all of the living circumstances in stride. In fact, she blossomed in the environment. She was one of a select few chosen at The International School of Lusaka to attend the model United Nations Conference in Nairobi. She traveled with a group of students and spent a week with students from all over the world discussing matters of importance to their generation. You could not find parents any more proud of their daughter than Donna and I were. She had talked a lot about deciding that she was going to come back to Zambia after her education and teach. Now, it would be just the two of us until I could complete Ana's adoption, finish building plans, and get us home.

The next few days were anxious ones. I found that trusting God for my family's care wasn't easy. I had trusted my church to do the right thing, and look at what happened. So many questions continued to assault me, the whys never had an answer. The greatest question beginning to haunt me was; How could God be in the middle of all of this?

It would take Donna and the girls two full days to get to Chicago. From that point we had no idea what was going to happen. Would they stay in Chicago? The first of February can be bitterly cold. And they got on the plane not even having a coat to wear. Doubts began filling my mind. Questions and second-guessing were drowning my ability to think. Did I do the right thing in sending them home? I was impotent in stopping the attack on Donna. Now, I wasn't about to stand by and let another thing happen to her and our family.

The third day after their departure Donna called on the phone. It was good to hear her voice. She sounded tired and confused. That kind of travel is very tiring, and when you travel that far with two children, it is exhausting. Add to all of that, the extreme stress they were under. Donna arrived in Chicago physically exhausted and mentally dazed. In a state of shock would be a better way to say it. Her brother was waiting for her at the airport. She told me that after a couple of days in Chicago they would go north to Wisconsin and stay with him.

All of the events the previous week went by like they were unreal, like I was watching things from a distance take place all around me, like I was detached. My own trauma was making things difficult for me. My mind wasn't clear enough to even think about tomorrow.

A couple of days after Donna left, some of our friends came into Lusaka. They were stunned at the news of Donna, Hilary, and Ana having to leave. There was no chance to say goodbye. No time to give a hug, to recall, and laugh at past good times. No time to embrace people that you loved and cherished as your own family. One of my personal regrets in having to send them home was the emptiness left in their hearts. Goodbyes and hugs are so important, and my wife and two of my precious children missed out on both. What was I supposed to say to people that asked about Donna? Should I tell them that because she was attacked by a man and abandoned by her church she suffered a breakdown? Tell them I had no choice but to send her home? I was lost for answers.

It took me some time to get my bearings. I tried to put my priorities in order. Gradually, I came to know what I needed to get done. The most important task was to complete the paperwork for Ana's adoption. Next, I needed to complete a couple of rural building projects. With those items taken care of, I would have to make all of the arrangements to get home. It was going to be a lot bigger job than just getting a couple of airline tickets. All of our belongings that I didn't give away or sell would have to be shipped. Other missionaries might want some of our appliances.

Up until the day Donna left, she cried at the thought of losing Ana. So, I knew that completing Ana's adoption was crucial. When the Zimbabwean woman told Donna that if she wasn't careful she would go home without Ana, it terrified her. She would rather die than lose her child. In Lusaka I stopped by the office of the Director of Child Welfare, we set an appointment time and I left. I had met him before and he explained to me a little about adoption in Zambia.

I arrived at his office at the right time and explained to him the circumstances we were in and that I needed to complete the adoption process as soon as possible. He explained what I would need to submit to the government and told me it would take his department about six months to provide the required paperwork. He must have sensed my disappointment, so he told me that if I was willing to type up all of the documents, it may take as little as four to six weeks. I assured him that I was more than willing to type every last word that was needed. We both had other business to deal with, so we agreed to meet in two days.

When we met again, he handed me about twenty sheets of lined yellow paper. On front and back he had written out every word that I needed to type. The documents were: the Petition for Adoption, the Consent for Adoption, and the Order of Adoption. God was helping me through this wonderful compassionate man. He told me that even before our first meeting he had heard about Ana and her miraculous recovery. I spent that Friday night and all day Saturday at the typewriter. We weren't fortunate enough to have a computer. In fact, I was fortunate to have an older IBM electric with an extra typing ball. Well, when Saturday night arrived, I had more than forty pages of required documents typed. What a tremendous feeling it was to have it done. And I thought, I didn't do too badly for a hunt-and-peck typist.

On Sunday, Donna telephoned. I told her that I had all of the documents done and ready to turn in to the court. I needed to reassure her that nothing was going to happen to take Ana away from us. She told me that they were at her brother's in Wisconsin and it had been snowing. Ana was having a ball playing in it. Whenever she wanted to go outside to play, she would ask somebody to help her put on her "snow snoot." It was so good to hear Donna's voice. She asked me how long it would be before I could bring Marily home and we could be together as a family. I told her it was still going to take a couple of months. After a tearful, "I love you," we hung up. I felt empty inside, like I was some kind of a shell. I felt like a puzzle with pieces missing.

a wonderful day

^^^

I thought this day would never arrive. It is March 13, and this is the day baby Harriett will become Ana Syoma Galloway. As I wait for the judge, my heart is thousands of miles away with Donna. She has been back in the states for about six weeks. She is safe with Hilary and Ana. They are living at the church camp just north of Grand Rapids. The same loving shepherd that bid us farewell a couple of years ago opened his arms to take Donna and the girls in. I know she wishes she could be here with me on this miraculous day. Lord, how many nights did Donna fall asleep holding onto Ana, praying for a miracle? How many tears ran down her cheeks as she was praying for Marily and me thousands of miles from her? She deserves to be here with me. She should be able to watch the judge stamp the papers. Lord, I wish she was here. I wish we were together on this day. We would celebrate and have a party. We could reflect together on your graciousness to us.

The assistant to the judge arrives and escorts me to a small office. The room's furnishings are sparse. A small desk and old oak chair on casters occupy one side of the room. Only two other chairs share the rest of the space. The assistant has all of the documents I typed and submitted. I was so privileged to have the gentleman from the Child Welfare Office help me. I am glad I listened to him and we did the paperwork together. I was a little familiar with the government's processes. Most Zambian offices are an administrative nightmare.

The door to the office opens, and the judge enters the room, I stand to greet him, and we exchange a warm handshake. I have met him before. He is a wonderful Christian man, a member of the Zambian Bible Society. He asks me some questions about Ana, and I tell him the miraculous story of her life and God's hand upon her. As we continue our conversation, I can sense that he is grieved. He tells me how his spirit hurts because of the darkness many Zambians still live in.

He tells me his court is beginning to prosecute cases of tribal or traditional murder. He explains about traditional murder, incidents in which the life of someone is sacrificed because of village or tribal superstition. As a case in point, he tells me about a recent situation. One of the tribes in the north and north central regions was lost in a very evil superstition. If a child's two front top teeth are the first to come through, then the child is evil. The doomed infant is wrapped in his or her chitangi, tied to a rock and thrown into the river. I wonder how people can live in such darkness near the end of the twentieth century. And then I recall in our own land we sacrifice infants before they are even born. As he talks, he is passionate about the need for the light of the Gospel to shine in his country.

Our conversation comes to a close, and it is quiet. The judge asks the assistant if the proper papers are in order. The assistant tells him that every document is exactly as it should be. He takes a cursory look at the papers and places each document in a separate place on his desk. He opens a drawer and places his stamp and pad on the desk, right in front. From a different drawer he takes out his imprinter with his seal on it. In a very respectful way he places the seal on his desk as well. I look at my watch; it is 9:13 a.m. My heart is pounding; my eyes are misty. The stamp thumps on the pad and then stamps "The Order of Adoption." It is totally impossible to put into words how I feel at this moment in time. Days and nights of concern, praying, worrying, doubting, fearing our little girl might be taken from us, first by death or ignorance, and just recently by evil intent, are gone. Those excruciating moments are blown out of my spirit, just as winds sweep across the beautiful savannah.

With that last stamp and his seal our little one becomes Ana Syoma Galloway. She is God's special delivery to a family of Americans who have been privileged to love and be loved. The seal and stamp are the official acknowledgment of what has been taking place for many months: God's love lived out in a mother who never cared about the color of skin. My dear wife can now rest assured that her Zambian angel is a part of us in name as well as in the bond of family. As I leave the office of the judge, I am lost for words, and our handshake tells what words can't. I feel that a tremendous burden has just been taken off my shoulders. With the adoption completed, now I can begin the process of going home.

going home

∧∧∧∧

With Ana's adoption completed, I could now concentrate on going home and being with my family. Donna was so happy when I told her, "Ana is now our child." And with the adoption complete I began to realize just how much energy it had taken out of me. The mental and emotional toll was adding up. For a couple of days I felt depleted, running on empty. I knew that I had a lot to do before we could leave. I would need to wrap up as many projects as possible. The projects I couldn't finish would have to be left for someone else to do. There were no plans to replace me in the immediate future, so some things might not get finished for a long time, if ever. I couldn't worry about that. I had enough on my plate. So for a couple of days I worked on a detailed explanation of my responsibilities and the projects not completed.

As Marily and I prepared to leave, most of the people around me acted like everything was fine. Here I was, walking around like my soul was missing, and the staff of people all around acted like nothing had happened. It was as though my family was just a mark on a calendar, a date to be forgotten. If it wasn't for one or two friends who stayed by my side, the last days would have been much darker and colder. I questioned God again: Why did we come to Zambia? What possible good can tip the balance when weighed against the evil and heartbreak dumped on my family?

Again, like so many times these past three months, I was without answers. Oh, I knew in my mind, because of my theology, that good was recorded in heaven. But it did little or nothing for my soul. It was not helping Donna. It couldn't help Hilary, who was left with so many questions in her heart; she left with an aching heart because she never had the chance to say good-bye to people she loved. The more I thought about why we came to Zambia, my mind finally settled on one little life. Maybe, just maybe, we waited those ten long years and traveled to a remote land to be blessed by one tiny struggling life. Well, Lord, if Ana was the reason, then all of the garbage these past few months has been a small price to pay. As I settled on this thought, a sense of peace began to help me. What price are we willing to pay to love and continue loving, even when the cost is high?

On the practical side, I had to ship our belongings home. To do so, I would need to build a couple of shipping crates, which I didn't want to do until I knew how much stuff was going home and how much was staying behind. I decided that I would give away as many of our household items as I could. So, I gave to our workers and their wives our pots and pans and dishes. They loved it because most of them had only one pot to cook in and a very limited number of plates or bowls. I had a great time giving it away. I even decided to give away all of Donna's Tupperware. You would have thought I was passing out gold bars. I gave all of the Tupperware to two of the women who had been good friends with Donna. I was amazed at how thrilled they were with the gifts. I had more fun giving things away than I had had in a long, long time. Every item, no matter how small or insignificant in my eyes, was received with joy and gratitude. I gave something to each of my workers, something different, and something they could put to good use.

I had decided that I was going to do something a little special for the young man who drove my children to school and drove my wife on her many missions of mercy. He was a pretty tall young man who wore about a size ten shoe, and I had a pair of good-quality leather work boots, with steel toes. Even though they were two sizes too big, he was so excited when I gave them to him that he danced around. His smile displayed the joy in his heart.

Our final days in Zambia were drawing to a close. I was told that around the first of April I could make our arrangements to go back to the states. At this point I had just a couple of things to take care of, and then it would just be the waiting. A few days before leaving, the administrative staff held a farewell luncheon for us. This was usually done when someone left. We gathered at the fellowship room and had lunch. After eating, a couple of people were selected to have some words of farewell. My heart was thousands of miles away, and because of all that had led up to our decision to leave, I didn't care about the get-together. I thought it was a bit of a sham, just another way to keep things looking normal. In truth, though, things would never be normal again, never.

Yet despite the hardships and profound disappointments in how things had worked out, the prospect of leaving left me strangely ambivalent. The south of Africa still enthralled my soul. I was about to leave a land I loved and people who were my family. The images of the villages and little children, of the sun setting behind the giant Baobab, were a positive addiction to me. The people, the smells, the poverty, the smiles, all of it had crept into my soul. And now I had to say goodbye. Nothing these last few months seemed fair. My entire family was near collapse. Something inside told me that the toll of the past months would be staggering, almost crushing, and we would face many more battles.

our descent into the abyss

∧∧∧

arily and I gathered at the airport with a couple of friends.
The goodbyes were all done, the tears were shed, and it was
time to leave the land that we loved. At this point, I was
not much more than an empty shell. The stress of the previous days and
weeks had left me drained of energy and very troubled in my personal
faith. Again, the knowledge in my head did little to lift my spirits or
sooth my soul. When I sat down inside the jet, I wanted to go to sleep.
And when I woke up, I didn't want to remember anything since New
Year's Eve, that day that changed everything.

The flights seemed to take forever. The minutes seemed like hours.
There was no excitement in my soul, only fatigue and questions with
no answers. I couldn't wait for the wheels to touch down at Chicago's
O'Hara Field airport. I knew Donna and my girls would be waiting
for us. Marily and I cleared Immigration and Customs as quickly as
possible, and as we passed through the gates; three beautiful, smiling

faces were waiting for us. The long weeks of waiting were finally over. Now I was hugging and kissing my wonderful wife. Hilary grabbed me around the waist, and then I picked up my beautiful gift, Ana Syoma. It was so nice to see and hold onto them. When I picked up Ana, she hugged my neck and said, "My Papa." It felt like my heart was melting inside me. Hilary looked so happy to see us. Her smile always made me so happy to be her dad. Marily passed around hugs and kisses and we were finally home, together.

We left the airport and headed back to the apartment Donna had been given. After showering and getting settled, we went out for dinner. It was so nice looking at my family together and smiling. We would have to stay in Chicago for a couple of days. There were some meetings we had to attend; they were supposed to bring us up to date on current church and administrative changes.

Near the end of those meetings we met with our denominational leader. He oversaw the work of our denomination in eleven states. When we sat and talked with him, it seemed as though he was ignorant of what really took place. He kept referring to the attack against Donna as "The Incident." I asked him about any correspondence he received from London describing what happened. He told me that he had received a fax informing him that Donna and two of our daughters had to come home immediately. And that was the extent of any information that he had. Our meeting ended, and then we were able to take a week's vacation.

On April fourteenth, we would need to be in our new church. We were told by our soon to be district director that the church we would be moving too was in need of our leadership and experience. He told us that the congregation was having some serious relationship conflicts.

With a vehicle loaded we left Chicago and headed to Northern Michigan and Grandma's house. It was early April, and there was still snow on the ground, so our activities that week were going to be pretty limited. We did some shopping for new clothes and visited with our family. It was a fast week, and I don't think I had the chance to even begin adapting back to life in the states. I thought that we needed three or four weeks to readjust, but we were told that the church needed us as soon as possible. So, with our week over and wanting to forget the past we headed to Mid-Michigan.

We arrived in our small town on April fourteenth. We settled in at the house, and Donna went about trying to make it like home. The house was just behind the church, so going to the office was going to be very easy. I thought that getting busy would be good for us, so we dove right into the work. The congregation numbered about thirty to forty on any given Sunday. The people were friendly and greeted us with open arms and expectant hearts.

The pastor that we followed had severe marital problems and had been unfaithful towards his wife. The pain and deep issue was the fact that his adultery was with a very young woman in the church. The mother of the young woman had given her consent for the relationship in hopes that a marriage could come out of it. So, upon understanding all of this we knew that we had a lot of work to do to bring the people together.

Since Marily had graduated from high school in Zambia, she was now enrolling in the state university located a few miles north of us. She wanted to get her degree in world history and literature. Her intention was to go back to Zambia, or some other country, and teach in the Cambridge International School System. We enrolled Hilary in the public school just a few blocks away from the house. Ana, well, she was the joy of everybody who met her. Her smile and sense of joy were infectious. At two and a half she was walking perfectly normally. Her badly bowed legs were as strong as possible. She played and ran like she owned the world.

Because the house was so close to the church, we had very little privacy. The backyard was open right to the church property as well. So, that spring I decided to build a fence around the back yard. I wanted Ana to help and knew that we would have fun together. So as I built the fence, with Ana by my side every second of the project. She loved carrying the cordless drill. At some rather easy places I even let her drill in a couple of screws.

We poured ourselves into our ministry and witnessed God bring about healing in some hearts and a few new people became part of the life of the congregation. Still, in our hearts we struggled in our small town. The feelings of incompleteness and loss were always with us. Hilary experienced a very harmful confrontation in the public school with a male student who was two years older than everybody in class. It brought a lot of fear into Hilary's life. So we voiced our concern for Hilary and some friends introduced us to their friends whose children attended a Christian school. We met with the teacher, and he warmly accepted Hilary and us. Her fees were waved in lieu of our performing janitorial duties on a rotating basis. Hilary responded pretty well to the new school, and she made good friends, which brought a sense of relief to us.

Our stay in that small town lasted two years. I have to admit that I kept myself as guarded as possible with the people. I was battling so many issues and traumas that I had no intention to increase the heartache. The last official goodbye was in Zambia and I was still suffering, and so was Donna. Again, it was time for goodbyes and moving on. Prior to leaving we had our last meeting with our volunteer board. After lunch and farewell all of the members left but one. Roger stayed behind. He was a very caring and sensitive man. We chatted for a few minutes, and he prepared to leave. Well, as he did Ana came up to us and told us she needed to have a group hug, like Barney always did. I picked up our little angel, and she wrapped her arms around Roger as we group hugged together. He left us with some very moist eyes and I imagine a rather tender heart.

Our new appointment was in Macomb County. The work in this appointment was extensive. I was responsible for a staff of more than twenty employees. The administrative work alone kept me busy. Being busy was good for me, I didn't have time for unproductive memories. The busier I was, the less I could think about Zambia.

Donna's and my marital relationship was hurting. We were both detached. We were detached from our own emotions and from each other. The best way to describe my emotional life was, "dead man walking." I didn't know how long I was going to be able to keep going. I felt like a hypocrite on Sunday mornings. I would stand in front of the congregation preaching on the love and faithfulness of God, when deep down in my soul I felt unloved and abandoned. I felt my church abandoned my family by not standing up for the truth, and God had certainly left us out in the cold by allowing all of the trash to be dumped on us. Even at this low point I had no idea that our darkest hours were hurtling toward us.

I found the bottle of laxative tablets by accident. I saw them on the floor under Hilary's bed when I moved it one day. Donna had been trying to tell me that she was afraid that Hilary was in trouble. She thought Hilary was suffering from an eating disorder. I didn't want to believe it. Why would my little girl want to hurt herself? Why would she want to do this to her sisters and us? Now I was holding the bottle in my hand, and I began to understand that my daughter was in serious danger.

When we showed her the bottle, she denied that it was hers. She told us she was holding them for a friend. She denied that she was having any problems at all. We didn't know what to do. She had been losing weight. She continued to lose weight, and her eyes were getting very dark and her skin pale.

A short time after this, the youth group from church was going to a small carnival that had come to town. While they were at the carnival, Hilary collapsed. At the hospital the doctors told us that her heart was not beating in the right rhythm. She was anorexic, and she had damaged her heart. She was put in the cardiac intensive care unit. This couldn't be happening. Hilary was my Joyful Light, which is what her name meant.

Donna and I had planned on naming her Amanda. That changed the very instant I held onto her for the first time. I was at Donna's side during the c-section. I sat and watched as the doctor performed the surgery. I loved every moment of it. I was enthralled with the whole thing. I talked with Donna the entire time, telling her exactly what the doctor was doing. As the doctor delivered our new daughter, he handed her to me. I held her while they cut the cord. I was holding in my hands the most beautiful form of God's creative genius that existed. I told Donna that we would have to name her Hilary Ellen, our Joyful Light.

Now I stood by her bedside. She was very pale, and her eyes were dark and sunken. The beeping of the monitor was the only sound that I heard. Every time the line on the monitor jumped, my own heart wanted to stop. I had watched and marveled at her birth, but now I stood numb, broken, heartsick, as I watched her almost die. The doctors told us again that her heart had been damaged. After a couple of days of intensive care and monitoring, they were able to stabilize her. In four days we took her home with a heart monitor.

God, what is happening to us? How much more can one family endure before we are fractured, broken beyond repair? Donna and I talked for a long time and made the most difficult decision ever in relation to our daughter. We talked with our family doctor, and he recommended we call a local hospital that specialized in the care Hilary needed. I called the hospital and answered some very basic questions. We agreed to bring Hilary in the next day. After making the arrangements, I phoned our regional office and told a fellow pastor what we needed to do. He told me that he would inform the regional director as soon as possible. Our hearts were so heavy; Donna and I cried and held onto each other for the longest time. We needed a friend so badly, and like a lot of other ministers we had just a few, and none close by.

We agreed that we would keep Hilary out of school the next day. We would explain to her what we felt we must do for her health. I had a twisting knot in my stomach. My soul was so heavy I felt like I was being crushed. I didn't sleep that night; the minutes were filled with questions that could not be answered. Those awful minutes passed tortuously.

The morning came and I felt weighed down even more with the knowledge of what we had to do that day. When we talked with Hilary, we told her how worried we were. She agreed with us that something was wrong. Just to have her acknowledge that helped me. The hospital was only about half an hour away. She packed a small bag, and we left the house. The trip was silent even though the radio played some contemporary Christian music. The music did little to ease the knot in my stomach or bring peace to my soul.

We arrived at the hospital and parked. There was no one around as we entered the front lobby. I pressed a buzzer, and in a moment the intake person arrived. We introduced ourselves, and Hilary began the intake process. After the paperwork was done, we were buzzed through a security door. I was beginning to feel that this was not quite what I thought. The intake person suggested we leave and let her get settled by herself. Donna and I both kissed her goodbye and turned to leave. The next words that I heard cut through my already wounded heart, "Daddy, please don't leave me. I promise I will get better. Please, Daddy." With tears streaming down my face I could not look at Hilary as she uttered those words. I turned and walked out the door. The heavy steel door closed, and the metallic sound of the latch echoed behind us. Donna and I were locked out, and our Joyful Light was locked in.

We walked to our car in the parking lot, collapsing into our seats we cried like babies. God where are you? How can you allow any more to happen? Do you want us destroyed, paralyzed, utterly broken and shattered? We can't take any more of what you're passing out! My soul was empty, and I had no answers. No answers, yet I was the one that people came to with their own questions. People looked to me countless times for comfort and understanding. Now I sat in the car with Donna, the mother of our precious children, and we both felt abandoned by the God we had given our life and service to.

We hadn't realized what it was going to be like for Hilary. She had to wear a hospital gown and slippers. The doors were kept locked at all times. She would not be allowed to use the pay-phone until she earned enough merit points. Needless to say, her first weekend was one of loneliness and fear. After the weekend we went to see her. It was then that she told us what it was like. We asked her if she would see a counselor if we took her home. She agreed, and we signed her out. When we told our doctor about what it was like, he apologized. When he spoke to the hospital, he was told that the hospital deals primarily with mentally and emotionally troubled children and adolescents.

The very next day we made arrangements with a nationally respected Christian counseling service to begin seeing Hilary. She began to see a wonderful Christian woman twice a week. Her counselor was young, and Hilary began to trust her. We never asked Hilary what she talked about. She needed to know that she could trust her counselor and say anything to her. It would be weeks before Hilary would open up to us. Slowly she began to express her pain and guilt. In her heart she felt guilty for not being with Donna when she was attacked. Usually Hilary was at her mother's side on visits that had to do with people being sick or hurt. She felt guilty that she couldn't control what happened to her mother or the trauma that the coming days would bring. She felt helpless and out of control. But she learned that the one thing she could control was what she ate and how she looked.

I really woke up the day I watched her monitors beep and scrawl their jagged and jumpy lines. I had wanted to deny all of the anger and other emotions I had kept inside. There was a lot of anger consuming me, anger towards the man that wrought havoc on my family. I was angry at an organization that did absolutely nothing to protest what happened. The deepest anger was for me. Anger for not seeing it coming. Anger for not being able to protect my wife from her attacker. And anger for not being able to protect her from the comments and innuendos made by others. We heard what people said about us. Why we failed as missionaries. Why Donna had to be sent home.

With all of the stress it was impossible for us to be good pastors. Both of us hurt so bad that our pain smothered us like a collapsed tent. Our peers all but abandoned us. We came back from Zambia different people, and I suppose the change made us uncomfortable to be around. In many respects, we had become isolated, and we longed for some way to break free of the chains of depression and despair.

a place for a new beginning

‹^^^›

With all of our struggles piling up, I thought I was going to collapse. I was numb and operated mostly out of habit and requirement. Because I was drowning and close to emotional death, I could not minister effectively to other people. I began to understand that we were not going to recover as long as we stayed within our denomination. Our natural tendency and determination would be to try, and try, and try some more. Yet, all of the time we would be getting further and further from recovering. At every turn I found myself questioning an administration that I didn't trust. I began to see that we needed to resign and try to breathe some different air.

Through this very dark time we continued to have a bright spot in our life, Ana. She was a constant source of blessing and encouragement. Her physical recovery was so complete it amazed us. During our struggle with Hilary and our own relationship, it was Ana who kept us walking towards brighter days. We enrolled her in school and looked forward to her first days in kindergarten. On her first day of school Donna and I walked her down the street to the corner where she would catch the bus. We held hands as we walked. When we got to the corner I taught her "The School Bus Song." I had taught it first to Marily, and then to Hilary. Now I was singing it to Ana. She caught on real fast as I sang it to her: "The Bus, The Bus, The, B-U-S." As we sang, the bus pulled around the corner and came to a stop in front of us. The big yellow bus, with its hissing air-brakes, opened the door in front of Ana. Without an instant of hesitation Ana Syoma marched up the steps and entered a world we prayed she would live long enough to see. The bus door closed, and Ana waved goodbye. That morning a mom and dad wiped away some tears as they turned and walked home.

Hilary began to show some small glimmers of recovery. She was very faithful in her commitment to keeping every appointment with her counselor. As well, Donna and I had been seeing our own counselor for a while. At times, it seemed like we were learning to cope. At other times the wounds would open, and our recovery would swirl down the drain, like drops of blood washed down the bathroom sink. On one of the appointments with our counselor Donna and I came to the same conclusion that we should resign as ministers. We both knew that we were unable to serve to the capacity we wanted. We knew that as long as the wounds were left untreated, we would continue to bleed. The most devastating sense we had was this: our administration was not protesting what had happened to Donna in Zambia. We came to feel that we were, in fact, *persona non grata*, and that it would be better for them if we just disappeared from the scene. If we were gone, then they could forget about what happened.

We explained to Marily and Hilary what we thought we needed to do. Marily was going to college, and we wanted her to continue. Hilary wanted us to do, in her words, "whatever it takes for you to be happy again." Donna and I began to pray in earnest for God to lead us to a place of healing, whatever and wherever that was.

An answer for our prayers was already being prepared. It was sometime in February when we made the final decision to resign. We knew we needed to talk to Donna's mom about what we had to do. We didn't want her hearing some rumor about us. About the first of March we took a week's vacation and headed north. We had time to talk with Donna's mother, and she was very supportive. She knew we were struggling, and something needed to change. While we were up north, we went to visit our friends who owned the apple orchard. We had a great dinner of northern Michigan surf and turf; walleye filet and venison steak. Few things could make us feel more at home.

After dinner we talked about life's uncertainties. As a couple our friends were both facing some pretty challenging circumstances. He had severe heart problems, and she was in an accident that almost killed her. It left her with debilitating neck and back problems. His heart problems were so bad that he was unable to do the work in the orchard.

He knew what had happened to us, and he expressed that we were not the same people who had come out to the orchard almost five years earlier. During our conversation he asked us a question that floored us: "How would you like to buy the orchard?" We had no idea that he was trying to sell their farm. Their physical difficulties were forcing them into the decision. He talked a lot about how he was trying to move his family and the plans that were in motion. And then we talked about the timing of God. We agreed to pray, and if God opened the doors for us, we would buy the orchard. We left our friends that night after prayerfully committing the entire situation into God's care.

We knew that we needed to make an appointment with our area leader and discuss with him our intention to resign. When we met with him, we discussed how we felt about our ability to serve and shared our conclusion that it would be best if we resigned. Our conversation did not go very well. After explaining how we felt, he abruptly and dismissively said, "I never ask people to stay. If you want to quit, then go ahead."

Whatever we had expected from that visit, like understanding or sympathy, it certainly wasn't what we got. We left his office and set off to prepare our letters of resignation. Now after all of the heartbreaking situations we had dealt with, we were now on a course to leave the ministry we loved.

Just days later, an event took place that deepened my conviction we needed to leave. Donna spent a week in the hospital with stroke-like symptoms. The first couple of days were pretty scary. The doctors determined she had a series of T.I.A.'s. These are episodes in the brain that can be precursors to more severe problems. The attending physician told us that these were probably triggered by the stress that Donna had been living with. I felt pretty sure that if we stayed and continued to struggle Donna's health would crumble. We definitely needed a change.

And that change was in the making. We got a phone call from our friends up north. All of the arrangements for their move had come together. He wanted to know when we could come to make the formal offer on the orchard. As it worked out, we went north on the weekend of my birthday. So, on my birthday, sitting at the kitchen table at the farm house, we made a formal offer for the orchard. The real estate agent was there with the papers, and we signed the purchase agreement. Our friends accepted an offer from us which was 65 percent of the listed price.

I had been doing a lot of thinking about how things seemed to be working out. We were going to have a place of our own for the very first time, a place to begin again, a place to breathe different air, a place to allow time and God bring healing. After some thinking about the orchard, I came up with a fitting name: Genesis Farm, our place of new beginnings.

Marily was doing very well at the university and wanted to stay behind. We talked with my brother who lived just a few miles away from the campus. He had room and gladly welcomed Marily into his home. It was so reassuring to both Donna and me to have Marily staying at my brother's place. She would fit right in, and family would bring peace to her soul.

god's zambian speedster

∧∧∧

*L*ate that spring we moved to Genesis Farm. I began to take care of the orchard right away. My friend's heart condition had kept him from some of the important routine tasks of orchard maintenance. He hadn't been able to keep up with the pruning for a couple of years. This spring he wasn't able to spray the orchard for early fungus infection or insect prevention. I had to play catch up with the sprays and take what came. I decided the coming winter I would have to heavily prune one third of the orchard, and do the same for the next two winters. That would get the trees back into shape.

I prayed every day that this move would help us sort things out and find some peace. The nights on the farm were so quiet; we were more than nine miles from the small village at the east end of our road. Some nights a car wouldn't come by for hours. During the stillness of the night we would sit outside under the canopy of thousands of small twinkling diamonds. The night sky and the stillness reminded me of the bush.

Many nights at the farm we would gaze at the stars and listen to the local canine chorus provided by the coyotes. I loved to listen to them as their yips and shrill cries moved through the night. Some nights their singing came from a cedar swamp not far from us, and other nights they raised their voices in the hardwoods not a quarter mile away.

That summer Donna and I got pretty good jobs. She was working for the university extension program, and I was working part-time in an elementary school's youth risk program. Ana was soon to start second grade. Many times I looked at her and marveled at how beautiful she was. The school year started, and we were trying to get into the groove of living in the country, taking care of different responsibilities. This was very different from what we were used to. In our ministry just about everything was provided; your house, your cars, and your utilities. Now we had to handle all of it. At times, we felt out of place and not equipped for what we needed to do.

A few weeks into the school year we were contacted by Ana's teacher about a difficulty Ana was having. She felt Ana was having comprehension problems and wanted to have her tested. We agreed, and a team from the district, including her teacher, met with us to discuss the test findings. They were all in agreement that Ana was having difficulty in knowing how to put words together, even simple two-syllable words. They told us that unless she was put into a special program she would continue to have problems. Wanting to avoid special education, Donna asked what we might do to help. We knew the stigma attached to children who had to attend special education classes. We were told that if we read to Ana and had her read to us at least an hour to an hour and a half every night, she might overcome her difficulty.

That was all Donna needed to hear. From that day on for over a year we read to Ana, and she read back to us. Donna was the one who read with Ana the most. She was so determined that Ana was going to be able to read and understand, nothing was going to stop her. That fall and into our first winter they never missed a night in their reading time. By the time the snow was beginning to fly, Ana's teacher was noticing small improvements in her reading.

The holidays were wonderfully quiet. We had been so used to running seven days a week in the holiday season that by the time Christmas arrived, we were exhausted. This Christmas we helped out some with our pastor in town and really celebrated Christmas. We always liked things simple, and that was the way we were living. The girls got a few presents, and we enjoyed being together. Our life had a good appearance on the outside, but few knew the real story. Only a handful of family members knew exactly what happened in Zambia.

I was sitting at my desk at school when the phone rang. It was 9:20 in the morning on January 22. The voice on the other end of the phone was that of a friend who watched Ana when she got off the bus. She told me that she had just heard on the fire scanner that our house was on fire. I raced out of the school and headed home, a trip that usually took about twenty-five minutes.

When I arrived at the house, the local volunteer fire department had been on scene about twenty minutes. For a while it seemed that the brave men might get the fire under control. Then the wind shifted and blew the flames back toward the part of the attic that was not insulated. That was all it took. The flames roared through the rest of the house in a matter minutes. Our farm house, built before 1920, was now crumbling down. Donna arrived just as the entire roof was collapsing. Belongings from almost twenty-five years of marriage turned to ashes. The precious pictures and art work from each year the girls had been in school, turned to ashes. Donna's magnificent collection of baskets from Zambia turned to ashes. Her baskets were made by a woman with no fingers on one hand and just a stub for a thumb and a partial finger on the other. For days and weeks she worked in the leper village making those beautiful baskets for Donna. Now they were ash and muck and vapor.

It took all day for the firemen to clear the house. They had to be sure that the fire was completely out before we could go into what was left. The next morning Donna and I went out to the farm to look over what was left. People who have had a major fire will tell you that some very strange things can happen inside a fire, which we discovered as we were going through the remains. For example, boxes of candles were next to some music CD's in the kitchen. The plastic cases for the music melted together, yet not a foot away the candles never even began to melt. Another example: In our bedroom the ceiling caved in, causing some drywall to fall on our bed and nightstand. The drywall covered one of my Bibles, and it remained in very good condition. The only sign of a fire on the Bible was the black smudge in the burgundy leather that was not covered by the corner of the drywall.

That morning we found another interesting sight, this one worth laughing about. In the back mudroom of the house we had an old refrigerator that we used when needed. That Christmas we put an extra turkey in the freezer compartment. Well, that morning as we looked through the few remains of our earthly belongings, we saw the turkey was lying in the snow close to where the back door would have been. The turkey was completely cooked; it even had the little button popped out telling us it was done. The refrigerator must have acted like an oven cooking the turkey a beautiful golden brown.

A few days after the fire some very dear friends let us move into an empty house that was in the family. They agreed to let us stay there until spring when we would have to rebuild our home. The winter months went by very slowly. I tried to go out to the orchard each day after work to keep up my scheduled pruning. Donna continued very faithfully with Ana's reading. Reading was always such a big part of our family. Before Marily had finished elementary school, she had read several hundred books. Hilary was a good reader as well. I read the C. S. Lewis classics to the girls when they were small. Their imaginations were filled with word pictures of Narnia, The White Witch and, of course, the majestic Aslan. In fact, Donna was convinced that Marily and Hilary both read so much because she had read to them while they were still warm and secure in her womb.

We managed to get through that winter and all of the stress that goes along with losing a home and dealing with an insurance company. We were looking forward to spring and the chance to tear down the remains of the house. Its ugly charred skeleton had stood out like a blemish on the beautiful snow-drifted countryside. With the coming of spring Donna and I decided on the type of house that we wanted. We decided on a Cape Cod style home with natural cedar siding. It would be all finished for us except the upstairs, that we would have to complete ourselves.

As the school year was coming to a close, we were anxious to hear from the school their final thoughts on Ana's reading comprehension. We knew she was doing better because her frustration level with reading was much lower than at the start of the school year. Well, Ana's teacher and one of the professionals who tested her told us that she had improved tremendously. He felt that she would probably struggle with reading, but if she worked hard, she would do fine. So Ana's second grade year was very eventful and stressful for her, but she braved every challenge, and her determination grew even stronger.

By midsummer the house was up, and we were planning on getting settled in. When we moved to the farm, there was a basketball hoop attached to the pole barn. I didn't pay much attention to it because it was kind of hard to play ball on gravel. When I was much younger, I used to shoot around in the driveway. In fact, I must confess I had a pretty good jump shot. Ana wanted to play some ball with me, so I decided I would try to teach her to play "horse." She picked up a ball, and before the end of summer she was dribbling pretty darn well on the gravel. That in itself was quite an accomplishment. Gravel, especially big gravel, is tough to dribble on. If the gravel is mixed with some clay, the surface can be smoothed out. But there certainly wasn't much clay left in our gravel. With the side of your foot you could pile up the rocks pretty easily. The ball would shoot out in any direction as it glanced off the rocks.

Ana seemed to love having the ball in her hands. Every free minute she was challenging me to games of horse. It was so funny the first few times she tried to shoot the ball. With all of her might she would shoot, and if the ball hit the rim, it was a big deal. It was so much fun out in the driveway with her. She would never quit, no matter how tired she was. If I was willing to play, she was right out there with me.

With the fall coming Ana was starting the third grade. We were so proud of her. Her reading skills had improved, and her teacher remarked at how hard she was working. She was doing well in all of her subjects. In October, she wanted to join the area-wide girls' basketball program for third through sixth graders. Her school was going to have its own team of third and fourth graders, and Ana wanted to play. We were so excited the first time we went to one of the schools where the games were played. Ana's skill at dribbling was pretty amazing. After she learned on the gravel to control the ball, I showed her a couple of other drills. She would practice with her eyes closed. She worked on dribbling going from a standing position to sitting on the floor without stopping. She was becoming pretty good.

That fall and early winter we learned something wonderful about our little girl. Not only could she dribble a ball, she could dribble and run flat out, faster than anyone else on the court. She practiced every day and played games on Saturday. We would all go to watch her play. We took Grandma to the games as well. After each game, we would go out and have breakfast. Ana loved to have her Grandma come and watch her play. It was a wonderful time for us to be together.

Ana progressed well through the third grade. Her teachers were always telling us how polite and hardworking she was. Spring and then summer came, and Ana's third grade came to an end. That summer Ana and three of her friends entered a three- on-three basketball tournament. There were about ten teams in her age bracket, so there was a lot of competition. The first day of competition they won their games. The second day would be elimination games for the championship. I told Ana that if her team placed in the top three I would get her a trampoline. Well, they did, and the next day I found myself putting together a trampoline.

Ana continued to practice on the gravel driveway and play ball every chance she got. Through elementary school I had the joy of coaching her and her friends in the fourth and sixth grades. She continued to study hard, and her grades in school reflected her determination.

It was hard to believe, but now our little girl was on her way to junior high school. It was a big change going from a country school to the much larger junior high school, but Ana adapted well. It seemed that wherever she went, she made friends. Her smile and joyful spirit were magnetic. Ana played ball that year, and the team did very well. Again, we heard so many encouraging words about how fast she was and how well she could control the ball. More than once I had tears in my eyes as I watched her play.

The summer after seventh grade we moved from the farm. I had accepted the invitation to pastor a small church about twenty miles away. The church had been without a pastor for a couple of years, and Donna and I felt it was the Lord's leading. The decision to move was very hard on Ana. She had made many friends and had been in the same school system for seven years. Marily and Hilary never had that opportunity as we moved almost every three years.

By this time Hilary had met a wonderful man, Tim. He was a veteran paratrooper who was hurt when his chute collapsed about 150 feet from the ground. He was discharged and moved back to Alpena. Hilary and Tim met, and the rest is history. They married and moved into the farm house. They were both going to college, and this was the only way we could help them.

So we settled into our small town. We registered Ana for school and asked about the girls' basketball program. We were told that practice for the eighth grade girls would begin the first full week of school.

Starting in the new school was hard for Ana. She was a very shy child at heart. The school and classes were very small, and almost all of the students had grown up together and formed their friendships very early. Quite a few times Donna would encourage Ana by telling her, "Be friendly, and you will make friends." Slowly, she began to talk about the friends she was making. When we could hear her talking to her new friends on the phone, it made us feel better and brought a lot of relief to my heart.

When the school year began, Ana joined the basketball team. They practiced after school every day. The first couple of weeks were very difficult for her. It seemed that the girls on the team had been playing together since elementary school. So, not only did Ana have to fit into an already tight team, but she had to learn the various offensive and defensive plays that the girls had learned the year before. A few of the evenings when I picked her up, I could sense her frustration. A couple of times she even talked about quitting. It didn't take long, though, for her stubborn determination to kick in, and then there was no stopping her. She played well that year and earned every minute of playing time the coach would give her. Of course, I have to admit that for a while I thought she deserved to play a little more. But as we watched her play, we were gratified to hear the same words about her: "Man, that little girl is fast. Look at her dribble that ball!"

After the basketball season Ana and a few of the girls wanted to continue playing and practicing. After talking to a couple of other parents, we decided to form an A.A.U. team, so the girls could play through the winter. They practiced hard and traveled almost every other weekend during the winter months. The experience was good for them because they played against teams from much bigger schools. As far as the won-lost column? We all tried to ignore it.

During the winter we were informed that Ana was going to be eligible for membership and induction into the National Junior Honor Society. We were so proud of her we could hardly contain our joy and happiness. She sent in all of the papers, and we had to wait to find out the results. The results came in the form of an invitation, an invitation to her induction. It was going to be held in the auditorium during the day and followed by a banquet that evening. It would be impossible to describe how we felt that day. Here was our little girl being recognized for her scholastic and citizenship achievements. With God's hand upon her life and her spirit of determination, she banished forever the pronouncements of mental and physical difficulties. With every academic success, the words of doom were cast out into unreachable space. With every pass made and point scored on the court, any words or thoughts of physical infirmities were blown away like leaves in the autumn wind.

That evening we got dressed up for the banquet because we wanted Ana to know how proud we were. Naturally, she thought the suit and tie were a little too much, but we attended the induction and the banquet with grateful hearts. Grandma was able to come to the banquet, a special treat for her. When they called Ana's name at the induction and handed her the certificates, a mom and dad couldn't really see very well. For some crazy reason their eyes were kind of watery. The banquet went well, and we enjoyed watching Ana interact with her friends.

The following spring Ana decided she wanted to run on the track team. Donna and I were excited for her. She began track practice, and we looked forward to her first meet. The practices were hard as the team had to run miles and sprints each day. Track practice also started at a pretty nasty time of the year. Spring in northern Michigan can mean anything from fifty degrees and sunny to blinding sleet and snow. I told Donna it took a lot of guts to be outside running around the school to get into shape.

After a couple of weeks of workouts the season began. On the day of her first meet Donna and I stood at the track field, watching and waiting. The meet was against a school about the same size as ours. Ana was scheduled to be in three events: the 70 and 100 meter dashes and the 400 meter relay. In the relay event she was to be the last runner, the anchor. There were not a lot of girls, and it was hard to judge their ability without having seen them compete before. Ana herself had never run in a meet before. In fact, near the end of the practice regime, she surprised us by saying she hated to run. Nevertheless, here she was, and so were we.

I hadn't been to a track meet in a long time, and I forgot that the running events took place after all of the field events. It was over an hour into the meet when the announcer made the third call for the 100 meter dash. Standing at the finish line, my stomach was in knots. I had butterflies so bad it hurt. I always got a knot in my stomach as I watched the start of her basketball games. And now the butterflies were doing a dance inside of me. From my view at the finish line, it was hard to distinguish each runner, but I could make out Ana's position. "It is only a race, so why am I so nervous?" I asked myself, hoping to calm down my nerves.

The starter raised his hand, and I heard the crack of his pistol. Instantly the teammates from both schools started yelling and cheering. The noise began at the starting line and moved down the side of the track with the runners. I was straining my eyes, trying to distinguish who was ahead. Close to the fifty meter point, I could see that Ana was in second place, about one stride behind a runner from the opposing team. Ana was running hard, yet I could tell that she was not giving it everything she had.

At the end, the other runner crossed the finish line about a stride ahead of Ana. She placed second for her first event ever in a track meet. Her friends gathered around, congratulating her. But I could tell from the look on her face she was not very happy. I met her and gave her a big hug. She said she was upset because she did not get

a good start at the line. She said the other girl was a stride ahead of her from the very beginning. I encouraged her to focus on the starter and to block out everything else at her next event.

A short time later, I heard the third call for the 70 meter dash. The same girl who won the earlier race was running this race, too. Again, my stomach was in knots, and in my head I spoke as if to Ana, "Concentrate on the starter, and block everything else out of your mind." Suddenly, the gun cracked, and again the cheering erupted, flowing in a wave down the sidelines as the runners progressed. Leaning as far as I could over the fence at the finish line, I could see Ana was in the lead. As she closed in on the finish line, her friends yelled, "Go, Ana, Go!" She finished first, well ahead of the other runner.

I could tell that she was giving it every ounce of energy she had. She was not about to finish second place again. With a time of just ten seconds, people were amazed at how fast she was. I smiled, and I thought God must be smiling, too.

The last event of the meet was the relay. It was past 6:30 p.m., and the teams had been out on the track since 4 p.m. It was easy to see the kids were tired and wanted the meet to be over. The announcer made the final call for the relay, and the runners took their positions. The relay is a team event that requires a lot of practice and determination. The hand-off of the baton must be done as fluidly as possible so as not to lose time. The hand-off must also be done within a certain distance in the team's lane. If either runner goes out of the lane or the hand-off is not completed within the required distance, the team is disqualified for the event.

Ana was running the anchor position. The runners before the anchor either give the anchor a little cushion, or the anchor is the one who must catch up. I was watching as the girls took their places, again with knots inside my stomach. The pistol cracked, and the runners were off. Our girls started off well, our first-leg runner was ahead by a couple of strides. The hand-off to the second runner was a little shaky, allowing an opposing runner to draw even. The hand- off to the opposing team's third runner was almost perfect, and she was well on her way. But our second hand-off was a disaster; our third runner dropped the baton in the exchange. She stopped, went back for it, and then ran as fast as she could. But the opposing team's third runner was a good ten meters or more ahead.

When Ana got the baton in the third hand-off the opposing anchor was already coming around the curved end of the track. I thought it would be almost impossible for Ana to catch her in such a short distance since both girls were running flat out. As her opponent rounded the bend and broke into my sight, it looked as though Ana might be gaining on her. With only 50 meters to go, Ana was just behind her. From the look on Ana's face, I sensed this race was one to remember. At 40 meters, Ana was just about even with her. The entire crowd was on their feet, everybody, those in the stands and those who had been just standing around.

From the finish line I was yelling, "Dig, Ana! Dig! Dig, Ana! Dig!" and dig she did. While her teammates cheered and yelled and jumped, my little Zambian angel tore across the finish line two strides ahead of her challenger. Her friends swarmed around her, giving her high fives and hugs. After I came back down to earth, my eyes caught a glimpse of Donna. We smiled at each other, at Ana, and at God, who has so wondrously blessed us.

A little while later when Donna and I talked, we knew in our hearts that any pain or disaster we had faced was insignificant compared to the joy and love we felt in our spirits and hearts whenever we looked at our Zambian angel. God did know what He was doing when He sent a simple American family to the beautiful Zambian bush. He did know exactly when a newborn would need a mother and caring sisters. He also knew of the tragedy and pain a family would deal with. He stood by us as a daughter came close to the door of death. He was with us as fire burnt to ash and vapor memories of beautiful childhoods. And He is with us today as we try as a family to demonstrate a simple, yet unfathomable truth: love.

epilogue

Ana was a member of the National Honor Society throughout her high school years. In addition, her relay team from track went to the state finals three years in a row. And, all of the work on the gravel driveway paid big dividends. She was the starting point guard for the basketball team for four years and was named by the *Detroit Free Press*, as Honorable Mention All State Point Guard. Her desire is to help people through non-profit work. She hopes that eventually she will visit the land of her birth.

Hilary earned her nursing license and hopes to use her skills to serve the needs of children. She is the mother of three wonderful children who attend church and are very active in the youth ministry. Hilary is still learning how to deal with her physical limitations caused by her anorexia.

Marily has worked for a banking institution for the past eleven years. She has just made plans to leave the bank and finish her degree in political science. Once completed she would like to attend law school and help those in need of counsel and service.

Donna is wonderfully blessed to be the pastor of a rural United Methodist Church. She dearly loves the people in her parish and they dearly love her. The folks in town have received us very warmly and she views the entire town as her congregation. Her love of God and joyous spirit have opened many doors and endeared her to many.

It appears to me that some people are able to choose the roads of life they want to travel. They make goals and plans and many times they are achieved. Some people begin their travels with plans and goals, and they gradually change and amend them. Still others travel down roads that suddenly end, abruptly leaving them perplexed, both about their pasts and their futures. My life, as well as the lives of those most dear to me, seemed to have come to such an end of the road that New Year's Eve.

The attack on Donna and the trauma and stress that followed made me sense that I was at the end of any path in life that made sense. These past years made me question everything, things I once felt sure of. Even my basic faith in God was in question.

We had been left in a fog; fog so thick that light couldn't penetrate. All of our life had been dedicated to serving; serving God, the church, and the needy. The treatment of Donna after the attack, in Zambia and in the states, made me think public image is more important than doing what is right. Doing the right thing is usually not the easy thing. It seems to me that easy and right are usually at opposite ends of decisions.

Leaving full-time ministry and moving to Genesis Farm put me in a place God would use. He began revealing to me truth about my own life. Truth I needed to understand. In His mercy he allowed me to see that pride can be a powerful intoxicant. Prior to our move to Zambia the denomination spent thousands of dollars to prepare us, mentally and materially. And, there were a few occasions when we would stand and receive recognition by hundreds of people.

As my peers were climbing the ecclesiastical ladder in the traditional way, I was taking another route. As a missionary who returned to the states, I expected I would be moved along to higher positions as my friends were. I can see now that being submissive to the hand of God was an acknowledgment in my mind, but not as much in my soul. The emotional and mental devastation left me feeling alone and powerless. I didn't think anybody cared, I didn't think I had any close friends. I wouldn't dump any more garbage on Donna, she was trying to survive herself. I was at a point of weakness that I had never experienced before.

I had put serving the church and serving God as one in the same. I am sure that there are also thousands of Christians who place God and their denomination on almost equal status. I heard from pastors across the states that they felt that serving God and their denominations were one in the same. Today, I am thankful that God has allowed me to see the difference.

I love God in a much deeper way than ever before. I desire to serve Him out of the love He has placed in my heart. I know I can serve him within my present denomination or outside of it. And, I have been blessed to speak to many congregations outside of my own. Today, my desire is to communicate to others the spiritual lessons that I have learned.

The single greatest lesson that I learned is rather simple: Love is costly. Love cost Jesus Christ his life. Love cost the Father the sacrifice of His Son. What does love really cost us? How much pain are we willing to endure in loving someone? These are questions that each of must answer and our actions will broadcast the answer to those around us.

We need to love each other as Christ loved us. I do not mean that we have to get along all of the time, that is unrealistic and impossible. But, the church has a long history of mistreating her own people. Any Sunday morning we have wonderful people in our churches who are the walking wounded. They have been bruised and hurt by unkind words and wrong judgments. Every church would be empty every Sunday if only perfectly righteous and holy people were allowed in. In fact, there would be no one to unlock the doors and turn on the lights. There would be no choir, no ushers, no teachers, and no preachers.

Jesus told us that the world would know we are his by the way we loved and treated each other. My prayer is that someday the body of Christ will be color-blind. That we will stop talking about loving people and simply demonstrate it.

about the author

Tedd Galloway is the fifth of seven children and the fourth son. His father served in the Pacific during World War Two. He grew up in the area south of Detroit known as the Downriver area. At the age of seventeen his parents, along with the three youngest children moved to a remote cabin in Northeastern Michigan. He graduated the next year from the area high school.

The following year, he met his future wife at a Youth for Christ roller skating event. A short time later he dedicated his life to Christ. Marriage followed and the desire to serve God grew within both he and his wife, Donna. After an intense period of education and training both were ordained into the ministry.

With two children he and his wife served three churches in Western Michigan. After a waiting period of ten years he and his family moved to Zambia on the African continent. For the first year they lived in the bush at a remote school/hospital complex. Upon returning to the states he served in three congregations.

A serious back injury, in which his spinal cord was damaged, forced him to resign from full-time ministry. In the hopes of finding personal answers he began writing about life experiences and questioning God. A dark and painful time brought new light and purpose. He has since been writing a blog and is building a website. A ministry has begun; A Servant's Heart Ministry, with the purpose of communicating the power of touch and love.

He can be reached by email at tedd@teddgalloway.com and would be glad to answer questions and respond to requests for prayer.